The Life of Tom Marshall

By: Jim Stumm

LIBERTY UNDER ATTACK PUBLICATIONS

Copyleft Notice

This book is covered by a BipCot NoGovernment License. Re-use and modification is permitted to anyone EXCEPT for governments and the bludgies thereof.

Further Use Permission: Please feel free to use, re-use, distribute, copy, re-print, take credit for, steal, broadcast, mock, hate, quote, misquote, or modify this book in any way you see fit. Sell it, make copies and hand it out at concerts, make t-shirts, print it on flying disks, or do anything else because intellectual property is a State based haven of the weak, the stupid, and those lacking confidence in their own ability.

Looking for your next read or listen?

1. **Adventures in Illinois Law: Witnessing Tyranny Firsthand** by Shane Radliff (Audiobook/Anthology)
2. **Adventures in Illinois Higher Education: Communist Indoctrination** by Shane Radliff (Audiobook/Anthology)
3. **An Illusive Phantom of Hope: A Critique of Reformism** by Kyle Rearden (Audiobook/Anthology)
4. **The Production of Security** by Gustave de Molinari (Audiobook)
5. **Are Cops Constitutional?** by Roger Roots (Audiobook)
6. **Vonu: The Search for Personal Freedom** by Rayo (Audiobook)
7. **Argumentation Ethics: An Anthology** by Hans-Herman Hoppe et al (Anthology)
8. **Just Below The Surface: A Guide to Security Culture** by Kyle Rearden (Audiobook/Anthology)
9. **Sedition, Subversion, and Sabotage, Field Manual No. 1: A Three Part Solution to the State** by Ben Stone (Audiobook)
10. **#agora** by anonymous (Paperback and Kindle)
11. **Vonu: A Strategy for Self-Liberation** by Shane Radliff (Paperback/Audiobook)
12. **Second Realm: Book on Strategy** by Smuggler and XYZ (Paperback)
13. **Vonu: The Search for Personal Freedom** by Rayo (Special Paperback Reprint/Audiobook)
14. **Vonu: The Search for Personal Freedom, Part 2 [Letters From Rayo]** (Paperback)
15. **Going Mobile** by Tom Marshall (Paperback/Audiobook)
16. **Anarchist to Abolitionist: A Bad Quaker's Journey** by Ben Stone
17. **Brushfire, A Thriller** by Matthew Wojtecki

Looking for a publisher? Drop us a line:
www.libertyunderattack.com

Dedication

TO RAYO, who walked this path before any of us thought of it, and to the freedom pioneers carving niches of personal autonomy in a world opposed to it.

Foreword

Three years ago, I came across Rayo's book, *Vonu: The Search for Personal Freedom,* by mere happenstance. I was definitely impressed when I read it; so much so, that we spent 6 or so hours discussing the strategy of vonu during our *Direct Action Series* on *Liberty Under Attack Radio.*

I put the book away for a few months, but continued thinking about the ideas Rayo presented in this book. I had come across an onslaught of freedom strategies and a unique way of thinking about the world. It took some time for me to process it all.

At that same time, I was trying to recruit Kyle Rearden to join *LUA Radio* as a co-host. He refused time and time again, and I realized there was a way to get two birds stoned at once (Trailer Park Boys reference). So, one night on a Skype call, I brought up the idea. The conversation went something like this:

"So Kyle, since you're being a prick and won't officially join *LUA Radio*, let's start *The Vonu Podcast.* There's literally no one else on the planet that can do this with me, so you don't really have a choice."

He probably sighed and responded, "Yeah, yeah, alright. I'll do it."

Over the next few months, we planned out the podcast, setup the website, and started recording episodes towards the end of December/beginning of January 2017. We didn't officially launch the podcast until the end of January 2017, though.

When that first podcast went up on iTunes and the other podcatchers, I was and wasn't surprised by the response. On one hand, I knew there were others looking for something different than what was out there at the time; or, if not something different, just something that got their attention, something that inspired them. We quickly garnered a niche audience, attracting many individuals who made comments like, "This is what I've been doing my whole life, I just didn't have the word for it," or "This is the strategy I've been looking for."

In Season 1, we focused on the philosophy of vonu, covering subjects like: comparative vonu (comparing/contrasting vonu with anarchic schools of thought); legal interstices (utilizing legal loopholes to increase one's liberty); controlled schizophrenia (the "mental condition" of being a citizen-serf); the servile society; collective movementism, mean-time to harassment (how vonuans gauge the efficacy of their vonu); and a couple philosophical articles by Rayo.

Season 2, entitled, *The Practice of Vonu*, shifted the podcast towards action, but only strategies Rayo discussed in his writings. Those subjects included: financial independent-early retirement, ethical enclave trading, free isles and freeports (along with case studies), intentional communities, local congregations (like the Free State Project, or, more aptly, Free Keene), crypto-anarchism (Rayo was an early cypherpunk, merely due to the fact that he was so privacy/security-focused), strategic relocation, country shopping, living on a sailboat, van nomadism, vonu home bases, food storage, freemates, avenging angels, vonuing in cities, and self-liberational media.

Our current season 3, entitled, *The Expansion of Vonu*, will be ongoing indefinitely, alongside our Intermission episodes.

Throughout the duration of the podcast, we had been archiving and digitizing any old vonu publications we could get our hands on. But, our archive was still quite scarce. I scoured the Internet and was able to get a handful or so, but the leads ran dry.

In 2017, I came across an individual named Wally Conger, who had been in southern California in the 1980s, attending "dinner parties" with prominent libertarians of the time. He was subscribed to a number of these old "zines" and recently sent me his collection – some 25 new editions of INNOVATOR, along with other unique publications.

Just a couple weeks ago, I also came in contact with Jim Stumm, the author of the "book" you are about to read. He sent me the physical copy of this publication and some others. He also volunteered to send me copies of anything he has, which is basically everything from the 1960s-today. This is absolutely huge in our chronicling of this freedom strategy, as well as Tom Marshall's life.

Speaking of Jim, I would like to thank him for all of his work over the years, both in the self-liberational media realm, as well as his efforts in archiving these newsletters. Since he published Rayo's book under the pen name Jon Fisher, I'm confident this podcast would never have been started if it wasn't for his contributions.

He also helped me greatly in a project I have been working on. Namely something like, "The Ultimate Rayo Collection." All of his articles laid out in chronological order in one massive collection. Thanks to the Appendixes at the end of this book, in addition to his chronicling of Rayo's known life (below), my job is much easier now.

So, where is vonu today?

It's obviously impossible to quantify how many vonuans there were when Rayo started writing, and up to and around his disappearance. My speculation is that there are more vonuans today, for two reasons.

First off, the proliferation of the Internet has exposed millions of individuals to the possibility of alternative lifestyles: the van nomad movement, the tiny house movement, the off-grid homestead movement, etc. Many of these individuals chose to pursue these lifestyles for reasons irrespective of ideology or politics. Some just saw the current economic situation for what it was and wanted something different out of their lives.

Secondly, the political climate here in the USSA and throughout the world is devolving rapidly. And, the best way to create more anarchists/vonuans is for the State to become even more tyrannical. As the hollow stone of freedom is bled dry, more and more will decide to leave the plantation. That's the hope, obviously, and that's what appears to be happening.

A couple of quick notes before I turn you over to *The Life of Tom Marshall*: first off, any time you see an "Editor's Note," that is Jim speaking. Secondly, there are two portions early on that contain speculation on Jim's part. I'm leaving those in here for the historical record, but the inaccuracies ~~will be formatted as such~~.

Coming across Rayo and vonu has drastically changed my life for the better. For years, I jumped from ideology to ideology, stumbling through the dark in search of increased personal freedom. It took a long time (relatively speaking) to exorcise my collectivist roots. Now, on the other side of it all, I have a clear path forward for my self-liberation; and I have the great honor of getting to pass this message of hope and freedom onto you.

I hope you will take up the mantle and begin your pursuit of self-liberation. After all, vonu is yours for the making.

Shane Radliff
July 2019
VonuPodcast.com

The Life of Tom Marshall

He was called the Mystery Man of the Libertarian movement (LIBERTY Magazine, Aug. 1987, p. 11). Tom Marshall, sometimes known as El Rayo or Rayo, invented the word & the idea of vonu, which means becoming invulnerable to coercion by living out of sight and out of mind of persons who would coerce you. Usually this meant hiding out in the wilderness, but vonu in cities was also considered.

Tom wrote about his ideas in many small newsletters. I have copies of most of them. I have edited collections of Tom's writing twice before, in the Vonu book, published by Loompanics (now out of print), and in my 27-page report, "Vonu Book 2, Letters from Rayo."

From the articles Tom published, we can get a good idea of his movements and activities for about 10 years. What I will do here is put Tom's reports of where he was and what he was doing in chronological order. I'll add some reasonable speculation about what he was doing before and after that time, although we know nothing for certain about that part of his life.

For some of us, libertarians of a certain age, Tom was an important and inspirational figure, even if we didn't entirely agree with his ideas, or follow his way of life. This sketch of his life will show that he was no armchair philosopher. He dared to live according to the ideas that he sincerely believed.

EARLY YEARS:
"I am a consulting engineer, 36 years old, no family." That's what he wrote in PREFORM #1, June 1968, p. 4. So if Tom was 36 in 1968, he must have been born in 1932. He never published a word about his early life, as far as I know. And I have no other information about it. But he was 20 in 1952, which mean he was draft age at the time of the Korean War. He never wrote about military service, never said whether he had or had not been in the military, or if he had dodged the draft. Certainly, the kind of person he was in the 1960s and later, he would not have volunteered. As an engineer, he must have graduated from college, so most likely, he was in college in the early 1950s. Perhaps he had a student deferment, or was passed over by his draft board. We don't know.

~~We also don't know where he went to college. He never mentioned that either. But since he never indicated any familiarity with any locale east of the West Coast, it seems reasonable to guess that he grew up & went to school, somewhere on the West Coast. The earliest we know of him, he is living in or near Los Angeles, so perhaps that's where he grew up. His known travels take him up and down the West Coast, from Baja to British Columbia and points in between, but never east of there.~~ [I have been informed, by someone who should know, that Tom Marshall grew up in New England before moving west. –Jim Stumm]

~~By "no family," he apparently means he has no wife or children. Whether he had parents living at this time, or other relatives, we don't know. He never mentioned them in writing, but he also never said outright that he had no such relatives. He appears to be such a singular person that one is tempted to think he might have been an orphan, but there is no actual evidence of that either.~~

In the 1960s and 70s, Tom thought a nuclear war was imminent. At the time of the Cuban Missile Crisis (1962), he told his employer he was heading for the hills, and immediately did so (according to Ben Best, in LIBERTY, Aug. 1987, p. 14). Other than that detail, Tom's life is a complete mystery before 1963. Some additional information might be available from public records, but I haven't used that resource.

FREE ISLES:

The first extensive information we have about Tom concerns his participation in the old Preform-Inform, the Free Isles Project. Tom looks back to that time when he writes in 1969:

"I was active in the original Preform which, from 1963 to 1965, was an advance-study group seeking development of one or more 'Free Isles." A Free Isle was to be an open commercial city with sovereign independence and complete liberty, constructed in the ocean, or on territory leased from existing nations.

"Preform did research and gave presentations to several hundred freedom-seekers, but stopped short of acquiring an island. From the beginning, we were all aware of difficulties in obtaining and defending territory, but believed we could overcome these. We had not anticipated, however, the growing restrictions on international trade and travel; trade especially vital to a Free Isle during its first decade. Threat of further restrictions and/or a major US depression cooled our enthusiasm." (INNOVATOR, A69, p. 7-72)

The newsletters and other papers I have from the original Preform give the impression that Tom was an active participant in their activities, but they don't reveal exactly what Tom was doing, with one exception. The Jan. 1964 newsletter says that Tom presented a paper: "The Case for Constitutionalism," at their Oct. 13, 1963 meeting. The August 1964 issue adds that this paper "describes some of the abuses that might occur in an attempted system of 'Competitive Dispute Resolvers" and presents some of the advantages of a constitutionally limited government which operates as an explicit monopoly within a geographical area." So this paper, expressing Tom's views at that time, apparently argued for minarchism and against anarcho-capitalism. More than that, I can't say because I don't have a copy of Tom's "The Case for Constitutionalism," although I do have the paper he was apparently responding to "Competitive Dispute Resolvers," a 14-page paper written by Gill Cantwell.

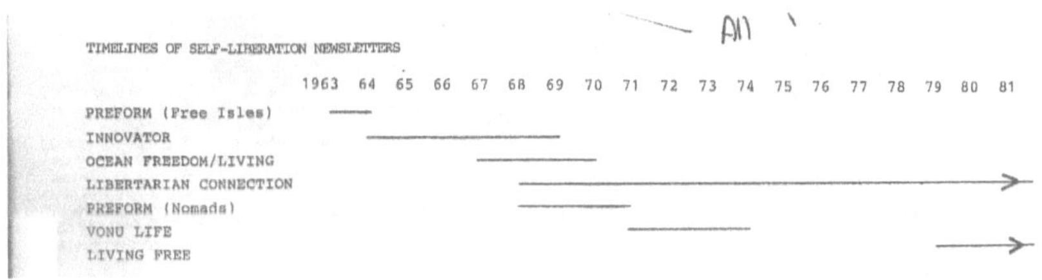

INNOVATOR:

In 1964, Preform became less active as many of the participants began devoting their time either to supporting Goldwater in the Presidential election, or to writing for and promoting INNOVATOR, a new libertarian newsletter that began publishing at this time.

Tom was a major contributor to INNOVATOR, but it wasn't his personal newsletter. In the beginning, the Forum for New Ideas is listed as the publisher, and Cara Leach is listed as the Owner and General Manager in the first issue and throughout most of 1964. In Nov. 1964, Konda Carter takes over as General Manager and Kerry Thornley is named as Editor. Through INNOVATOR's run, the colophon indicates that various people assumed different responsibilities at different times. From April to June 1965, Tom Marshall is named as the General Manager. From July through December 1965, Tom is Editor, according to the colophon. After that, El Ray is listed as a Contributing Editor, along with a number of others. The March 1968 issue does not list El Ray as the Editor for that issue. The April 1968 issue does not list El Ray or Tom Marshall in the colophon, but there is an article by El Ray in that issue. The next issue, Winter 1969, El Ray is once again named as the Issue Editor. Then the last issue of INNOVATOR, Autumn 1969, lists El Ray and the Gatherer as Issue Editors. It also appears that Tom wrote almost all of the last issue under various names.

In all, it appears that Tom wrote at least 46 full size articles, and a few shorter items, that were published in INNOVATOR from 1964 through 1969. He may have written others that were published under other pen names, but El Ray is the only pen name that I know for sure is Tom, and there are a couple "name withheld" articles that I strongly suspect were written by him. The written-by-Tom article count by year is: 1964-8, 1965-14, 1966-1, 1967-7, 1968-4, and 1969-12. His involvement with INNOVATOR is the only activity of Tom's that we know about for the years 1964-1967, with one exception:

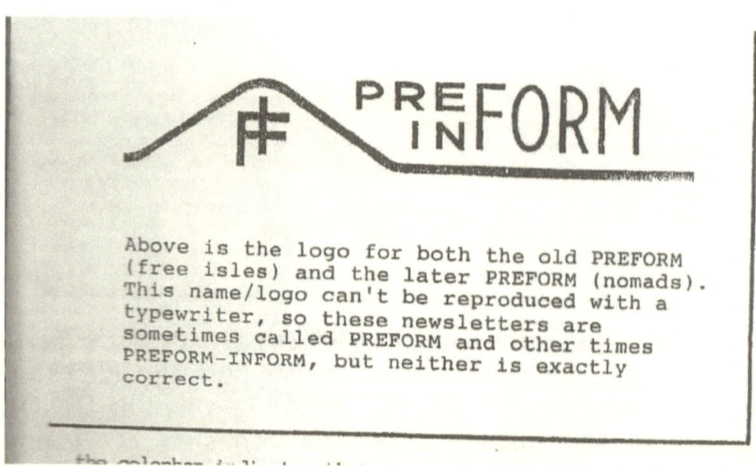

Above is the logo for both the old PREFORM (free isles) and the later PREFORM (nomads). This name/logo can't be reproduced with a typewriter, so these newsletters are sometimes called PREFORM and other times PREFORM-INFORM, but neither is exactly correct.

BELLA COOLA JOURNEY:

This is the title of an article by Tom Marshall that was published in the September 1967 issue of INNOVATOR. I believe this was the first article that describes his own activities. All previous articles by Tom or El Ray are either theoretical, or they describe interesting activities of other people.

This is a report concerning a trip he took to Bella Coola, British Columbia, Canada in late July and early August, presumably 1967. He drove to Bella Coola, which is a small town on an inlet of the ocean where the road ends. There he unpacked a folding kayak he had brought with him and he spent the next 10 days or so paddling along the ocean inlets and camping on beaches. He describes the features of the area in light of its suitability as a place for hiding out in the wilderness. He doesn't mention a companion, so apparently he was alone on this trip. That's all we know about his activities in 1967. The following years are better documented.

Bella Coola Journey

For wilderness retreats or summer anchorages, an especially attractive area is the North Coast of British Columbia – a land of snow-capped mountains, dense forests, rushing streams, and deep fjords. Its potential advantages include:

Ocean access: Myriad channels, arms and inlets – many extending over 50 miles inland – provide more sea coast than all of continental U.S. Among the almost endless inlets, bays, and islands are places a small boat could hide indefinitely.

Geographical isolation: Rugged mountain ranges limit transportation to water, which is slow, and air, which is expensive. Only two roads and one railroad penetrate the region.

Sparse population: The whole north Coast region (roughly from Queen Charlotte Strait to the Alaska panhandle and inland to the coastal divide) – larger than Ohio – has a population of less than 40,000, and most of these are concentrated around the few cities. Arable land and commercial timber exist only as small pockets in river valleys and deltas, precluding large-scale settlement.

In July and August, I explored some of the lands and waterways of this country. My route of travel was by automobile to Bella Coola, then by kayak to Nascall Bay on Dean Channel.

Although Bella Coola lies less than 300 miles from Vancouver by air, the highway distance is 650 miles. I first drove inland and north to Williams Lake, then northwest on a fair-to-middling graded-dirt road across the Fraser Plateau. Separated from the ocean by mountains, this three-thousand-foot plateau has a climate quite different from the coast – more like the higher plateaus of Colorado and Wyoming – mild summers, cold winters, and little precipitation. The road to Bella Coola crosses gently rolling land – open forests of lodgepole pine with some douglas firs, spruce, and aspin; an occasional creek or lake. Cattle ranching is the principle industry. The few small settlements have a "frontier look" – lob cabins, unpretentious yards, pole fences.

After 250 miles of little variation, the land changes abruptly as the road descends steeply with several switchbacks to the Bella Coola valley. Within a few miles, one plunges from the cool open woods of the uplands into a warmer, humid, dense jungle of giant arbor vitae and douglas firs. The road winds down the valley past a few logging operations and guest lodges. Then, 20 miles from salt water, the road becomes paved and wilderness is replaced by long-settled-looking farms and homes.

Bella Coola contrasts with the rough and rustic interior settlements, seeming (if one ignores the spectacular snow-capped peaks around it) more like a country town of the U.S. south than the trading center for thousands of square miles. The few businesses are scattered over a several block area; judging from the types of enterprises tourism is not an important industry. Prices are surprisingly low, considering Bella Coola's isolation and smallness as a market. A lunch consisting of a ham sandwich, pie, and milk cost about $0.70, a loaf of locally-baked bread sold for $0.26, and three pounds of powdered milk cost $1.40. (Prices are in Canadian dollars, which currently exchange for about 93¢ U.S.) Gasoline cost $0.48 per imperial gallon; equivalent to about $0.37 U.S. per U.S. gallon.

My boat was a 17-foot folding kayak, which weighs 125 pounds, complete with optional sloop sailing rig. I transported it to Bella Coola in disassembled form (parts less than 5 feet long), put it together on the banks of the river above town, and paddled downstream to the channel. The trip from Bella Coola to Nascall Bay took five days; four days were consumed struggling the 18 miles down North Bentinck Arm and Burke Channel against strong head winds and often white-capped waves. I traveled these waters only during the early morning when wind and waves were minimum; even the hard paddling netted only one knot headway. An attempt at upwind sailing in Burke Channel proved unproductive; the Folbot will go into the wind reasonably well in calm water but not when fighting three-foot waves.

Once beyond Bella Coola, the only signs of man were fishing boats (about a dozen a day passed), a couple of logging operations, and the remains of piers, log-boom, and cabins in some of the bays. The shores are mostly low cliffs with some pebbly-to-rocky beaches in the bays. On overnight stops, I either dragged the Folbot up a beach above the tidal zone (up to 15 feet) or tied up offshore. One of the most attractive camping places was a little cove (which doesn't show up on the land-status map) just northeast of Lalakata Point –

sandy beach, trickling creek, and hillsides covered with black raspberries and red bilberries.

On the fifth day, I passed Mesachie Nose, turned into Labouchere Channel and – for a change – had calm water and a light tailwind. With mainsail alone, I ghosted downwind to Dean Channel and then across it on an easy broad reach to Nascall Bay. Dean Channel was calmer than Burke had been, although a rain squall coming swiftly up channel caused some rough moments.

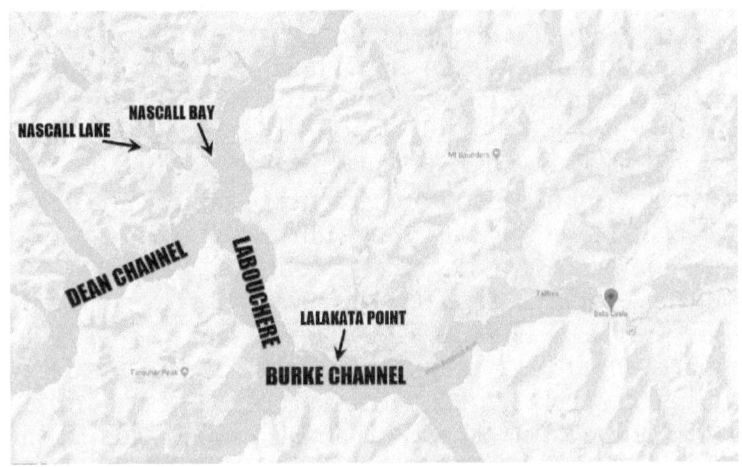

Half-mile-long Nascall Bay has the shape of an hourglass open on one end. A boat can anchor in the back portion out of sight of Dean Channel or the front. It is variously bordered by grassy, swampy, and rocky beaches and, in one spot, by sheer cliffs. Nascall Hot Springs lies near the mouth. Reportedly about ten years ago, Crown Zellerbach Corporation, which has a large pulp mill at Ocean Falls 20 miles to the west, surveyed Nascall Valley for hydro-electric potential. The survey crew built a bathhouse – a shack whose sole furnishing is a bathtub set into the floor. A pipe runs back into the hot spring. Since then, the bath has been used and fortuitously maintained by passing fishing and pleasure craft. During the three days I was in or around the bay, at least a dozen boats stopped.

On the return trip, I found a light northeast breeze down Dean Channel and sailed across to Labouchere Channel. There I encountered a light headwind. But with calm water and the wind following the zigzag channel, I made good headway with minimum tacking. Reaching Burke Channel, the sails caught the prevailing southwest wind and the boat was off racing the waves. Sometimes surfing on long swells for a minute at a time, sometimes crashing through short chop, the boat ran before the wind.

Comments on equipment: The basic Folbot proved to be sea-worthy, riding easily with the largest non-breaking waves encountered; under the same conditions, 40-foot fishing boats pounded heavily. With a waterproof kayak covering (which I lacked) to prevent swamping, I would trust it on the open ocean in average weather. However, the sailing gear has some design faults. A small outboard motor (available as an option) would facilitate cruising. Hip boots are desirable for travel along rivers and through swamps. A hand gun, although illegal in Canada, is much easier to carry through the woods (for defense) than is a rifle. One-sixteenth-inch netting will stop horse flies and mosquitoes but not the gnats which live on the coast (I encountered none in the interior). Several layers of loose clothing plus liberal and frequent applications of repellent on exposed skin kept the bugs at bay during the day. Insect pests are about as common as in more moist portions of the U.S.

At low elevations, forest grows everywhere except on naked rock, tidal flats, and swamps (any natural clearing in a river valley will be marsh, not dry grassland). Common species include: western hemlock, giant arbor vitae, sitka spruce, western white birch, douglas fir, yellow cypress, and black cottonwood plus on the more exposed slopes, the lodgepole pine. In the shade of some of the denser stands on delta lands, there is little undergrowth; elsewhere, it is heavy, and includes young hemlock, bilberries, ferns, mosses, smilacinas, and, in wet spots, devil's club. Rocks seen were exclusively igneous, many showing intrusions.

Palatable berries include blue and red bilberries, salmonberries, and red and black raspberries. The blue bilberry (Vaccinium avalifolium Sm) which makes up most of the undergrowth in many places, is related to and bears fruit shaped like blueberries. Bluebilberries are usually mildly sweet like a blueberry but some bushes (which look no different) bear berries which taste weedy or foul. Unlike raspberries, all berries on a bush ripen together and remain edible for a long time. Edible greens include plantain, fireweed, clover, ferns, and the various conifers. The only poisonous plants I noticed were water hemlock and baneberries (a few in swampy areas).

Salmon were running in Dean Channel while I was there. Mussels grow on some rocky beaches; near large rivers, the water is apparently too fresh. I did not see large game animals; perhaps they move to higher ground in summer. A few squirrels were encountered.

Due to the highly irregular terrain, coastal British Columbia shows great climactic variation – each river valley, channel, or inlet essentially has one or more local climates. A few generalizations can be made: summers are dryer and sunnier than winters, precipitation usually increases with elevation. But many anomalies remain. For instance, Bella Coola, at the head of an inlet, averages 55 inches of precipitation per year; Ocean Falls, 50 miles to the west and also at the head of an inlet, averages 164 inches; Bella Bella, 30 miles still further west and on a channel, receives 99 inches. Judging from plant maturity and comments by local people (weather stations being few and far between), Dean Channel has about the same summer weather as Bella Coola but a colder winter; it is more exposed to frigid northeast winds from the interior. One man said that the high precipitation and cloudiness at Ocean Falls is a localized condition caused by the shape of the valley; reporting that Ocean Falls would be overcast and raining for days at a time, while, eight miles away in Dean Channel, the sun was shining.

The most detailed map available (1) does not show terrain features smaller than a quarter mile. Aside from that, only a few discrepancies were noted, including, if the map be believed, a river which flows uphill (King Island, about Lat. 52° 17' N. Long. 126° 27' W). Perhaps this can be attributed to wishful thinking by the government's Department of Lands, Forests, and Water Resources.

During my stay in Canada, I was not molested by any large animals, not even the most vicious and loathsome of predators – the State bureaucrat. I camped out exclusively, not only in the wilderness but in relatively settled areas. During 10 days spent on rough waters in a conspicuously small, open, and unlicensed boat, a few passing fishermen solicitously asked if everything was alright; no Canadian equivalent of the Coast Guard ordered me off the waters. (During a one-day try-out of the Folbot on Piru Lake, Calif., I was ordered out for not having registration and local permit.) While many Canadian laws and regulations are as onerous as their U.S. counterparts ON PAPER, enforcement in an area with a population of less than one person per square mile presents something of a problem for even the most determined power seeker. The Canadian government will not sell outright any waterfront land; of course, this is to "preserve it for recreational use." But this poses no problem for the libertarian nomad who intends to only be a "squatter." TOM MARSHALL

URBAN ANONYMITY:

Before he took up van nomadism, Tom lived in a city, but in his own way. He describes the idea in general terms:

"The family lives in rented, furnished apartments or houses in a large city. Their means of protection are anonymity and mobility. Renting is done under an assumed name. They move every few months, leaving no forwarding address, and change names frequently. Their actual residential addresses are given only to trusted friends. Work is usually at a temporary job where he can arrange for taxes not to be withheld. They engage in free-market trade with libertarian acquaintances when profitable." (INNOVATOR, Spring 1969, p7-44)

About the same time, he mentioned that he lived this way in his reply to a letter in PREFORM:

"I went the urban, furnished-cottage rental route before going to truck-camper, which I recommend as the least objectionable of "conventional" shelters. It may be ideal for some, but I encountered problems – some reality, some perhaps psychological; nomadic living has solved most of these." (PREFORM #4, March 1969, p. 19)

Later, he described the idea again:

"The simplest approach to vonu in cities is anonymity: Be invisible, but not noticeable. Conform outwardly while doing your own thing in secret. Be inconspicuous. But a person probably should not do his own thing in his apartment. Renting under a "nom de plume" does not prevent inspection by landlord or police, or overhearing by nosy neighbors.

"It may be wise to avoid paying by check. But urban anonymity offers no protection from such dangers as nuclear war.

"I lived this way before taking up van nomadism. For me, anonymity alone was unsatisfactory because of city psychological pressures. I was immersed in an alien culture with values hostile to my own. Whether or not I was especially vulnerable, I felt vulnerable.

"I know of quite a few vonuists and libertarians who live this way, but I know of none who seem to like it for very long." (VONU LIFE #5, Jan. 1972, p. 4)

Tom's acquaintance, Kerry Thornley, recalls how Tom was living in the mid 1960s, and remembers the kind of person he was:

"Tom Marshall paid me a great honor. He informed me of the location of his home, a ramschakle cottage in Venice, and hired me to remove the throwaway newspapers from his front yard so as not to attract the curiosity of his neighbors while he was out of town in search of sites for ever more impregnable hideouts...His little house in Venice was just around the corner from a bar called Big Brother's..."

"People who feel warmth and affection for the character of Mr. Spock on the Star Trek television series might be able to imagine how much I missed Tom Marshall during that time I was living in Florida. In California, whenever I intuitively jumped to a conclusion, I used to share it with him, and two or three weeks later he would bring up the topic again, with a carefully reasoned, step-by-step, logical confirmation or refutation of my hunch. As plodding and conscientious as he seemed, his thinking processes resembled those of the computers with which he had worked with for so many years, and he never missed an alternate option nor ignored a contradiction." (NEW LIBERTARIAN #13, April 1985, p. 14)

Tom made a gradual transition from living in a cottage to living in a camper full time. He recalls:

"For several years before opting out, I carried food supplies in the trunk of my car, explored retreat areas, etc. What finally prompted my move was not "society" getting worse, but my own head getting better – disentangled from status and Statist games, plus more and better ideas on how to liberate myself." (PREFORM #9, May 1970, p. 16)

1968:

It was in the Fall of 1967 that Tom moved out of his cottage and began living full time in his camper. We get that date working backwards from what Tom wrote in June 1968:

"I am a consulting engineer, 36 years old, no family. For about 8 months, I have been living full time in a large camper. Utilities include cooking stove, floor furnace, hot-water heater, shower, DC-to-AC converter; all "self-contained." I use a trail motorcycle, which can be mounted on the back, for auxiliary transportation both in wilderness areas and cities. My mob assignments are temporary, lasting a few weeks to a few months; recent work has been in southern California. Between jobs, I usually stay at a "squat-spot" about 80 miles from Los Angeles...

"I intend to continue 'exportin' my labor for a while; topping off my savings so as to achieve a degree of financial independence. (Living as a nomad, expenses are low and saving is easy.)...

"I do not believe freedom is something that can be provided by "society" – certainly not by government. Each individual must accept responsibility for liberation himself...

"I expect to spend part of this summer working in southern California but hope to make one extended trip to Canada in July/August. I would enjoy meeting anyone with similar interests either in southern California or along my route.

"P.S. The typewriter and mimeo machine on which I prepared this are carried on board." (PREFORM #1, June 1968, p. 4)

Although it was signed "name withheld," the following was almost certainly written by Tom about this time:

LETTER FROM A NOMAD:

I am living in Big Tujunga Canyon. Bright sunlight and fresh air stream into my home. A hundred yards away rushes the creek. Beyond rise rugged hills, green with winter grass and budding shrubs. A few more days I will live here – writing, installing some equipment; then move to Los Angeles for a short, intense contract job. Next summer, when Tujunga Canyon is no longer very green and Los Angeles may be hot in more ways than one, I will be living somewhere in Canada. My home is a housecar.

I chose this way to freedom because it offers me the best of two worlds. I can live most-of-the-time away from regimented, congested, indefensible cities yet still profit by "exporting" my labor into these cities. I have the freedom and security offered by mobility; yet I possess what is in most respects a permanent residence. I can fully enjoy my life right now, yet live economically and accumulate capital for further ventures. Finally, I can "opt out" alone; while I look forward to trade with others who may choose similar or complimentary ways of life, my liberty does not depend on their decisions.

I am also delighted with unforeseen "fringe benefits"; ease of washing or resting after a journey; no worry about what to take with me; no time spent idle waiting for something or someone; no commuting to work. All travel is more efficient; I move only from destination to destination without intervening trips to a stationary home.

Far from having a primitive way of life, I enjoy electric lights, running hot and cold water, shower, gas range and heater. And all are "self-contained" – not dependent on external utility connections. With occasional refills of water, gasoline, and propane, I can enjoy my "modern conveniences" anywhere a rugged truck will take me.

At first I was crowded; especially when my rolling voluntary society doubled in population. But after consigning seldom-used items to storage, adding under-chassis compartments, and carefully rearranging, the interior is neat, belongings are accessible and space is adequate for two people.

Like many other self-liberating activities, mobile living is safest in the largest city or wildest wilderness. Cops have bothered me only twice in four months of living aboard; both times were in farming areas where, while traveling, I had stopped on (unposted) private land; patrolling deputies asked me to move on. I have no problems parking on city streets at night, usually in apartment residential areas. On jobs I often stay in the company parking lot. Only rarely have I rented space – the backyards of friends – when doing work which immobilizes the truck for several days.

This way of life is very economical. My almost-new housecar, including much gear I have added, has cost under $6000 – a fraction of the price of a comparable yacht or a well-equipped retreat home, not to mention a cracker-box in the suburbs. And living expenses for two total about $120 per month, including $55 for food, $20 for gasoline, $10 for maintenance, $10 rental for storage space, and $25 for miscellaneous.

So far I have been too busy to travel extensively or to seek out especially attractive campsites. But already I have lived many exquisite days and evenings at beaches, mountains and forests. I am still learning the way of a modern nomad, but already I am free. (INNOVATOR, March 1968, p6-1)

Above, Tom mentions his rolling society doubling, and rearranging his housecar so that 2 people can live in it, and living expenses for two. But this was published in March 1968. He didn't meet Roberta until the summer of 1969, as I will relate below. So this 2nd person, about whom Tom said no more in print, could not have been Roberta. It was some other unknown person. We can only guess that this must have been a relationship that didn't work out, that living in a housecar, or living with Tom, turned out to not be this other person's liking.

"El Ray" is named as the editor of the March 1968 issue of INNOVATOR. He wrote a brief introduction to that issue in which he says:

"This month, INNOVATOR turns to land mobility and nomadic living. An anonymous nomad describes his way of life. Tom Marshall surveys campers and trailers on the market. Don Stephens advises how to build your own for less. And Amelia Eiland and I interview the Proprietor-Scout of Libervan – a nomadic community that is fiction, but perhaps not for long."

SELF-LIBERATION SEMINAR, MAY 1968:
Tom writes in PREFORM #1:

I was a participant in Atlantis Enterprise's "Self Liberation" seminar held in Los Angeles this May. Five patterns of living for realizing personal freedom in the here-and-now were described & compared as to cost, freedom & safety for a "model" family of 2 adults & 3 children. These were: clandestine urban, underground shelter, remote homestead, land-mobile nomadic, & sea-mobile nomadic. The model land-mobile family was described thusly in the seminar notes:

The <u>LAND-MOBILE NOMAD</u> family lives in 2 campers. They have scouted & prepared a number of "squat-spots" at different locations but all on uninhabited non-privately-owned land. The family as a whole moves from squat-spot to squat-spot; the pattern of movement is somewhat seasonal. When funds are needed, one parent commutes weekly to the city utilizing the smaller camper for transportation & city housing. The other parent & children live in the larger camper which remains at the squat-spot, which is where the children are educated. For auxiliary storage they have caches & rented space outside the city. They do some foraging but, partly because of easy proximity of city work & stores, rely mainly on purchased supplies. Protection is through concealment while at the squat-sport, mobility when disturbed, & anonymity while traveling in the city.

I presented the land-mobility topic. Tracing the historical development of stationary residence, I hypothesized that the "industrialization" of agriculture had made obsolete attached dwellings for most of the population. I described the advantages of nomadic living & suggested ways to overcome the significant disadvantage: limited space. For the "model" family I recommended 2 self-propelled vehicles over camper plus trailer, camper plus tent, or single large vehicle. However the camper-plus-tent combination costs the least. For wilderness living I recommended selection & preparation of secret "squat-spots" rather than reliance on supervised campgrounds in National Forests. Suggestions for finding "squat-spots": Explore especially gently-rolling wooded land that has been logged; trees provide concealment & shade; water sources likely; a profusion of old logging trails can be easily improved.

In comparison with the other "self-liberational" modes as well as 3 "conventional" modes (urban rental, urban ownership, rural ownership), land-mobility rated lowest in overall cost in those situations requiring city employment. For present freedom & future safety, land-mobility is generally rated 2nd only to sea-mobility which is much more expensive.

About 30 people attended the seminar. One, a recent college graduate, has purchased a used delivery van which he is furnishing for full-time live-aboard. He plans to locate in Canada. (PREFORM #1, June 1968, p. 6)

In June 1968, Tom began publishing PREFORM for the purpose of "communication among libertarians and other freedom seekers interested in land mobility." He gave it this name because he had a large supply of printed letterhead with the Preform logo from the old Preform/Free Isles Project that he could use for 1st pages of his newsletter. PREFORM was typed and mimeographed with the typewriter and carried on board his camper, as Tom mentions above. The 2nd and 3rd issues of PREFORM were dated October 1968 and Jan. 1969. In addition, Tom wrote 4 articles that appeared in INNOVATOR during 1968. And "El Ray" was again the issue editor for the Winter 1969 issue of INNOVATOR (that is, winter 1968/1969). So he spent a lot of time during 1968 on these writing and editing activities.

1969:

In PREFORM #4, March 1969, p. 3, Tom provided some "background information on the editor" (himself):

"An engineer by profession, I have been an explicit libertarian for about 8 years; the most influential single book I have read is Ayn Rand's ATLAS SHRUGGED.

"Libertarian character references whom I have known for 4 years or more: Don and Barbara Stephens, Atlantis Enterprises; Kerry and Cara Leach/Thornley.

"Relevant, verifiable activities: active participant in (original) Preform – a laissez-faire freeport study group, 1963-1965; contributor to INNOVATOR (March 1964, Sept. 1967); general manager, then editor of INNOVATOR, April through Dec. 1965; lectured at Atlantis Enterprises' "Self-Liberation" and "Retreat" seminars in Spring 1968."

I notice that Tom lists only his INNOVATOR activities under the name of "Tom Marshall." He omits mentioning his additional extensive INNOVATOR articles under the name "El Ray."

Beginning on page 7 of this issue, Tom writes a long description of his lifestyle and attitudes:

I've been nomadic more than a year so most of the novelty has worn off – it seems natural. I recall several phases: inundated with the work of getting moved into the camper (plus some rented storage space); fear of unknown (will I be able to find places to park where I won't be harassed?); joy of liberation, almost like a perpetual vacation, celebration, FREEDOM; growing in freedom, growth pains (what do I do now?); press of mundane responsibilities that become part of a way of life, should tune up the engine, ought to put out another issue of PREFORM.

The only psychological problem I have so far identified is one not unique to nomadic living but encountered, I suspect, by almost every opt out, regardless of lifestyle: most of his life has been structured by other people & events; he has been told what to do & when to do it. Now, suddenly, he is largely free of all this. His life is all his to structure as he will. And this is a responsibility which overwhelms many people. I think this partly explains those who are loudly critical of the society around them, but firmly rooted, & who if propositioned will have no end of objections to ANY here & now self-liberation approach. Do they subconsciously sense their psychological dependency on some of the things they say they hate, & dread the thought of full responsibility for their own lives, no one else to blame for their shortcomings?

I still have nagging doubts about not accomplishing as much as I like as soon as I think I should. For example, some time ago I decided I should become a crack offhand shot with 22 rifle, & relearn to shoot left handed to use my better eye. I resolved to practice dry fire twice a day. But I haven't stuck to it. A Monday to Friday (plus overtime on Saturday) net builder would have all kinds of excuses to himself. But I haven't a one...

The tasks to which come off best are those which lend themselves to concentrated effort: I have been working on PREFORM, full time, 12 to 14 hours a day, for nearly 2 days now (amazing how much time one of these little sheets can consume) & will probably continue until I finish, then do almost nothing on it for several months until I put out the next issue.

I find I avoid cognitive dissonance more & more by cutting off dissonant communication: almost never read Establishment publications, rarely listen to the radio, & have no social relations with non-libertarians. On a job (consultant, part time) I limit communication to matters concerning work. I avoid most of the little day to day petty irritations of the Servile Society which are probably as important in psychological paralyzation [sic] as the big scary stuff.

I have developed my living patterns to the point where 2/3rds of my time is spent parked "in the hills" only 1/3 in the city. Right now, however (when I answered the letter), I am in a shopping center parking lot in Santa Monica, sorting out mail I just picked up, feasting on ground chuck & sherbet, which I can't store or gather in the wilderness. I was focused on correspondence until I introspected just now in response to this letter; I was rather oblivious to environment. I wonder if other shoppers passing the camper can hear the typewriter? If so, what might they think? (I doubt they hear it above the background noise; however I don't type late at night when in the city.)

(While publishing this issue of PREFORM, on the other hand, I'm at a squat spot along Coast Highway. It's on the side of a hill, old homesite, I believe; remains of a water tank with a pipe out of the hill, still flowing. Perhaps the people were forced out & the land taken by the govt, which has something not far away. It's been used a few times as a dump. It's less than a quarter mile from the ocean & highway; I can hear surf & traffic. Concealment seems marginal; the roof of my camper might be visible from a short stretch of the highway & at night I can see distant lights (Port Hueneme?), but I haven't been molested. I've been here total of 2 weeks on 2 occasions. Something which helps: the trail to the site is rather steep for the average auto; my rig has 35:1 low gear ratio & 2/3 of the weight on rear wheels. I bought some meat & fresh fruit when passing through Ojai several days ago, but that is all gone so I am back to staples, wild greens, & vitamin C. Wild mustard grows here, prolific with all the rain, I had a potful for dinner.) (PREFORM #4, March 1969, p. 7)

Roberta makes her first appearance in a letter in PREFORM #5, like many other letters in PREFORM, describing her ambitions:

"I'm interested in cycling across the US or Canada (trans-Canada Highway?). I'd like to take my time, earning money to finance me as I go along. I'd like to find someone else with similar notions. Know of anyone? -ROBERTA (Northern California) (PREFORM #5, May 1969, p.2)

In reply, Tom says in part:

"Before becoming a neo-nomad, I often camped out – from an automobile while traveling, sometimes backpacking, for 2 weeks from a folding kayak while exploring British Columbia fjords. The only significant disadvantage I found for this as a way of life (not just recreation) is that routine chores are more time consuming. In many ways, it is very attractive." (p. 3)

Later in that issue, he announces his plans for later in the year:

"I expect to move north about the end of May, visiting various West Coast environs, then summering in Central British Columbia. I will enjoy meeting nomads and other freedom seekers along the way or in BC (should you be summering there too).

"If you want to get a message to me quickly by mail, address it to PREFORM Attn Barbara Stephens. She will then open it and relay it to me when I phone in for messages. (Otherwise, it may sit for several months until I pick up mail.)" (PREFORM #5, May 1969, p. 11)

In the next PREFORM #6, dated September 1969, we learn that Roberta has become Tom's "freemate." Roberta recounts their meeting in a long letter on page 7:

"Only a few months ago, I was teaching in a state "gun run" school. It was my 1st, and I had decided, my last year of teaching in such a school. While at the job, I was thoroughly miserable and in search of a happier way of spending my life.

"Since I felt that the US Government was as bad as the Nazi regime had been, I was interested in a way of life whereby none of my earnings could be used to support a war machine. I had plans of going to Florida to work at a health resort in exchange for room and board as soon as my teaching contract expired (last June). That way I hoped to avoid income tax and also learn about natural hygiene. (My weight was a terrible problem and I had great hopes of reducing at this resort.)...

"While at my teaching job last fall I received from my mother a copy of "Vocations for Social Change." It's a Bay Area publication which lists among other things, the School of Living. I wrote to the School and subsequently subscribed to its newsletter THE GREEN REVOLUTION, also receiving its book, GO AHEAD AND LIVE. But even though I agreed with many of their ideas, the prospect of homesteading left me with some reservations: like who would feed the chickens and milk the cows and water the crops when I was on a bicycling trip? In other words, I viewed being tied down to a homestead just like that; being tied down.

"GR was exposing me to libertarian ideas however. And it was in GR that I saw an ad for PREFORM-INFORM which mentioned nomadic living. I suppose this appealed to me because I had dreams of getting on my bicycle and riding – destination the world. I'd be a bicycle gypsy. One of the PREFORM editions came with a hand-printed note on it from this guy who said he was going to British Columbia and would it be OK if he were to stop by and see me on the way. I answered and said sure, stop by. And that's how I met Tom and found out who is John Galt and a few other things.

"Tom came by on a Sunday. He stayed for the next few days. We exchanged literature. He gave me Rand's ANTHEM to read. It made sense and with Tom's help I was able to dislodge some of the cobwebs of prejudice that had been woven in my mind by an upbringing in a leftist family atmosphere. Thus I was able to accept and adopt much of the philosophy of that small volume. After the days had become a week, Tom asked me if I would like to go to BC with him. I thought about it and said "yes!"

"So when school was over and all my stuff moved out of the rented apartment I had been sharing with a friend, Tom and I were off to BC> Tom drove the 1st stretch – I shelled walnuts and asked a lot of questions. It was all very stimulating. While in BC at our forest squat spot, I read ATLAS SHRUGGED. I read it for breakfast, brunch, lunch, high tea, low tea, dinner, supper, and even by candle light. I loved every minute of it. Though I cannot meet the people in the book, I look forward to meeting and spending time with other libertarians as I would love forward to meeting John Galt, Dagny, and their friends...

"Right now, Tom and I are at a squat spot overlooking the Pacific Ocean. Since we are opposed to the State, its bureaucracy, and all of its trappings, we feel it is not in our best interest to have a State marriage license. However, Tom has drawn up on our own free marriage contract. Each of us is a "freemate." Also in the contract, PREFORM is a joint venture. Therefore, in the future, you'll be hearing more from this "freemate." ROBERTA (PREFORM #6, September 1969, pp. 7-9)

Two years later, Tom & Roberta published the text of their "free marriage contract" in VONU LIFE #2, July 1971, p. 5.

The heading of PREFORM from this #6 to the last issue, lists "Tom and Roberta, Editors."

They visited J.R. ROAF in Grants Pass, OR and he writes in PREFORM:

"Dear Tom and Roberta: Your surprise visit was a highlight and much in my mind for some time afterward -- -particularly with the June 1968 through March 1969 PREFORM. You are probably enjoying different sights and scenes and people – something new and different. Enjoy every minute of it...

"Your writing (both) is less reserved than conversation, perhaps because you did not know me and I am not familiar with the nomads and their language. The more I think on it, the less appeal it has for me; and the more I can see where others will find it satisfactory...

"As you said, Tom, "Nomadic living and agriculture don't mix, unfortunately." Food production is limited to hunting & gathering and following the harvests...

"Where I will locate is not known but I do favor some plan like M. Oliver's..."

Tom replies in part:

"New laissez-faire country projects I have heard of include M. Oliver's Capitalist Country and Project Atlantis. I have met and talked extensively with the proprietor of Project Atlantis and was highly impressed. He is a real-life Hank Reardon who has the capital to transform his dreams into reality.

"Strange your conclusion that agriculture and nomadism don't mix; you have about convinced me that they did. Roberta has been sprouting alfalfa seeds in glass jars (cover with nylon stocking material, rinse and drain twice a day) which supply our salad needs when we don't find time to forage." (PREFORM #6, September 1969, p. 5)

The proprietor of Project Atlantis was Werner Steifel (aka Warren Stevens). I wonder where & when this meeting with Tom took place. The headquarters of Project Atlantis was in NY state, near Albany. I don't suppose Tom ever visited there. We have no evidence that he ever traveled to the East Coast. More like Steifel traveled to California & while there, he talked to Tom, & perhaps to others as well who had been involved in the Free Isles Project, to gather information useful to his own New Country project. Operation Atlantis was no more successful than any of these other attempts at founding a new libertarian country that have arisen over the years.

Excerpt from a letter from R.I. VICTOR, Oakville, WA:

"While crossing Oregon via US 20, between Burns and Riley, I overtook a pickup-camper with a small motorcycle secured across the back of it – it also had a California license. If it WAS yours, it only proved the need of an insignia, significant to us, just another symbol to others."

Tom replies:

"We do regret not meeting you on our trip. We were already north of your when your letter giving your new address caught up. On the way south, we ran out of time (I had a work appointment to keep) and drove almost straight through. I don't think you saw us. We were traveling in a large truck-camper with LARGE (10" diameter) emblems on front and rear windows and smaller emblems on sides and motorbike. The emblem: gold crossed-F-I in green ring on a black field. Hopefully we will meet somewhere, sometime." (PREFORM #6, September 1969, p. 11)

Asked about nomadism as a defense again the SS [selective service] system (military conscription, Tom replies:

"Regarding safety from SS systems: In 2 years of nomadic living, I have been molested by police 2 times to the point of being asked to produce ID. I have not been arrested. This is less harassment by police than I experienced when living stationary, but not so little that I would unreservedly recommend my present lifestyle for draft avoidance." (PREFORM #7, December 1969, p. 11)

The Autumn 1969 issue of INNOVATOR (last issue) lists El Ray and The Gatherer as Issue Editors. The Gatherer or sometimes Dr. Naomi Gatherer, are pen names used by Roberta. Most articles in this issue appear to have been written by Tom under various names. Most are theoretical, about other people's activities, or how-to-do-it, but one, signed "Name Withheld," tells about his & Roberta's activities, without mentioning their names:

FURTHER REPORT FROM A NOMAD:

(Editor's Note: The March 1968 INNOVATOR, which explored van/camper nomadic living as a way of self-liberation, included "Letter From a Nomad." Here is a follow-up.)

My freemate and I are living in a secluded mountain valley about 100 miles from Los Angeles. Our home – a truck camper – is parked in an oak-pine forest, encircled by timbered peaks. At over 4000-feet elevation, we are enjoying brisk autumn weather – mostly warm, sunny days and cool nights. In another month or so, we will move to a low-desert site for the winter.

We have been squatting in this "National" forest – in the same spot – two months now, without permission and without trouble. About once a day, the King's men patrol the one maintained road – it is several miles away from our site – their truck tearing along at double the safe speed with horn blasting – commanding any peasants to get out of their way, like feudal lords of old. Otherwise this "public" property is left mostly to us "public," believe it or not. Sometimes on weekends we hear shooting in the distance. The few hunters that we have encountered on trails have openly, nonchalantly said they were hunting for deer – the deer season is long past. And many a "Smoke Here" sign put up by the forest fuzz gets ripped down.

But we don't leave self-protection to chance or to the whims of "public servants." We select and prepare "squat-spots" with freedom-loving care. We prefer rolling wooded land that was once logged over for its numerous seldom-traveled trails and countless spots a free man can hide.

At our present site, we are parked under two spreading live-oaks. These give adequate air cover without shading our south-facing solar-heating picture window. To our south, aircraft can't fly low because of the mountains. On the ground, our camper can't be seen beyond 50 years through the surround foliage. On our perimeter, we added dead branches to some of the prickly scrub-oak bushes to make natural-looking obstructions which encourage the infrequent hiker to go around rather than through.

The last half-mile of driveway we purposely left in rough condition: it took us two hours to traverse it, creeping in low gear – worth it for us, but not for the weekender or forest fuzz. A small station wagon which we use to visit the city is parked beyond the rough stretch; we hike in from there. Hiking trails, both for access and fetching water (we carry ten gallons about every other day from a creek 200-yards away) are separate from the driveway to minimize wear on the latter. On both vehicular and foot trails, we "arrange" intersections so that the more discernible and attractive forks lead away from our site. Sprinkling a few more oak leaves or pine needles (where these are the ground cover) does wonders to reduce signs of use. We find that with practice, our protection measures become largely automatic and require little more thought than keeping one's hand out of a fire.

I commute to work in Los Angeles about every other week. I sleep there in the station wagon, parked behind my place of work. I work as an independent contractor with no taxes withheld: I offer my client a lower rate in return for cash payment and flexible working hours.

Since I find it fairly easy to earn money, I have continued to do so. But as we grow more skillful in nomadic/wilderness living, we find we can live well on less and less money. We pay no rent and we travel relatively little (contrary to the average "serf's" idea of nomadic living). We eat what we forage plus bulk-purchased staples (currently wheat, brown rice, popcorn, soy grits, soy beans, lentils, powdered milk, vegetable oil, yeast, alfalfa speed (which we sprout), vitamin C and E tablets, and honey). We buy few clothes and these are wash-and-wear. Occasionally when in Los Angeles, we indulge in food and entertainment luxuries, but we enjoy these more as special treats. We stay out of status games.

Our range is not limited to Southern California. For two idyllic months, this summer we camped in the wilderness of central British Columbia – exploring, hunting, studying, and just loafing. We were parked on a sunny hillside above a roaring creek, with snow-capped mountains as a backdrop. We feasted on Saskatoon berries, red raspberries, squirrel stew, and an occasional grouse. One time a black bear visited us; another time a cow and calf moose wandered by, but not having an easy way to preserve so much meat in warm weather we let them be. We did not suffer from over-population: there were less than 100 people within a 50-mile radius.

We had no trouble crossing the border. When asked, we told the Canadian inquisitor that we were on vacation (giving fictitious place of employment) and would be visiting friends in Vancouver for a couple of weeks. We heard later that tourists who did not state a definite destination were turned back by the border guards because of the many forest fires.

Our rig consists of a medium-large, chassis-mount camper on a one-ton open-frame truck. Dual rear wheels, with front and rear wheels identical, eliminate need for a spare tire. The transmission is a four-speed manual with a LOW, low speed. With 70% of the weight on the rear wheels, in first gear, we can crawl into places otherwise accessible only with four-wheel drive. Even though the camper has full stand-up height and plenty of air resistance, we get 10 to 11 miles per gallon by limiting our cruising speed to 50 or 55 mph (we seldom need go faster). I have installed an extra gas tank, providing 55 gallons total capacity.

Present furnishings, many of which we installed ourselves, include stove with oven, instant hot-water heater, and floor furnace (all operating off bottled propane), a "demand" electric water pump and a 15-gallon water tank, shower, waste-water holding tank, separate 12-volt and 120-volt lights, a second battery and selection switch, and a surplus 24vdc-to-120vac converter which operates off both batteries in series. An ice-box came with the camper but this gets used for ordinary storage; with dry staples we don't need ice. For a head, we use the great outdoors when there; in the city, we use jars and plastic bags – simpler, lighter, easier to dispose of, and MUCH less expensive than any flush system. On the rear of the camper, I added under-chassis storage compartments plus a combination of bumper/trailer hitch/motorcycle mount. We use the trail bike for scouting and local errands.

While our California squat-spots would be secure in most "emergencies," we believe in extra "disaster insurance": well-hidden alternate identification, gasoline stores sufficient to take us to a far-off wilderness of our choice, a supply cache waiting for us there, and thorough familiarity with a certain unpopulated stretch of American-Canadian border.

When I became a nomad, I hardly expected every libertarian to do likewise. Many other lifestyles offer liberty. Then too, many people consider semi-slavery preferable to opting out. But I didn't expect the misrepresentation and hostility which has come from a few armchair ideologues.

As for self-liberation being a "cop-out" from the struggle against the State: we ARE confronting the State – and WINNING! We do (or don't do) pretty much as we choose, dress (or don't dress) how we feel, and trade in freedom with other free men (the few there are – so far). We are difficult to find and difficult to identify if found – practically unregimentable and largely untaxable. We, not the State, effectively control some choice land which the statists claim.

We don't believe that a "free society" will be brought about by a holy crusade to reform or destroy the Establishment, because we don't believe that altruist-collectivist means will bring libertarian ends. We refuse to sacrifice our lives in a futile effort to free millions of sheep-people who blank-out or fail to comprehend what freedom is, will not strive for liberation, and wouldn't appreciate liberty even if it were given to them. We do, however, encourage the incipient freedom-seekers we encounter – because we have strong self-interest motives: since so few are liberated, each additional free man means significantly more trade opportunities. If "society" ever is liberated, this, I think, is the way it will be done.

Some critics – who confuse liberty with utopia – say we haven't secured "real" freedom because we must defy threats and protect ourselves. But isn't eternal vigilance the price of liberty? Self-liberation DOES require a modicum of courage, self-confidence, initiative, and effort – more than does sitting in an easy chair spouting vague platitudes about "libertarian revolutions." Might this explain some people's reflex hostility?

Those who say we have abandoned civilization to slink off and live like animals are obviously misinformed. Our camper is truly advanced shelter; such innovations of private enterprise as plywood, aluminum, fiberglass, vinyl, and Formica make up a mobile shelter that is light and inexpensive, yet comfortable and durable. It is the "boxes" of city and suburb, big and little – built to conform to building codes 50-years obsolete, and unchanged in basic concept from barracks and huts of the agrarian dark-ages, which are primitive. As for "eating weeds," why shouldn't we, when they are as tasty, more nutritious, and often more accessible than the sprayed-and-wilted greenery of taxed-and-regulated groceries?

The delights of this way of life are not easy to convey. Nomadic living is like the perfect picnic, campout, or vacation – but more: we can scout and live in places which a vacationer – pressed for time – must pass up. And we have heat when it's cold, screens against insects, and hot showers when we get dirty; all the comforts of a house combined with the beauty and adventure of the wilderness. NAME WITHHELD

1970:
In a letter dated February 1970, Tom wrote:
I have never maintained that motorized-nomadism is a panacea. I did choose it for and have found it to be an excellent INTERIM life-style for someone still extensively involved in the servile society (through earning money, seeking a woman, etc.). I have always considered dependence on State-controlled highways and gasoline to be a major shortcoming, and a compromise I intended to rectify, which brings me to the main subject:

After much study and evaluation, my freemate and I have largely decided on a mix of troglodysm (underground) and pedestrian-nomadism as a FULLY LIBERATED (no compromises) life-style, into which we will evolve. Since nomadism and troglodysm intergrade nicely, this will be a gradual process. We will retain our camper indefinitely but as an ACCESSORY – secondary mobile home – to be sold or parked permanently if/when highway controls become appreciably worse.

For location we are considering areas from S Calif. and N. Cal. to interior B.C. One factor affecting location choice is access to other potential free men. (For personal self-satisfaction, we want to help build viable libertarian mini-culture(s); if liberation never gets beyond a handful of recluses hiding here and there, and libertarian philosophy died as they die, I will be disappointed.) And with less capability for long-range migration and increasing unreliability and restrictions of state postal, location will be increasingly important.

Our move toward pedestrian-nomadism/troglodysm is prompted in part by a feeling that we are not really free so long as we depend to any degree on legal interstices − including the State not (yet?) being as bad as the State could easily become. I want a life-style which can easily withstand the worst technocratic super-totalitarianism that is within the realm of reasonable possibility. We may still have some contact with That society but we won't have to worry appreciably over what idiotic thing the people-molesters do next (any more than somebody who takes a vacation at the Riviera now and then needs to be much concerned about the politics of France.) Our change in life-style will be, in a sense, an answer to the omnipotence-of-State line of Rothbard and Hess. We will answer not in words but by doing − the only real way. (LIVING FREE 19, October 1982, p. 6)

In the March 1970 issue of PREFORM, the masthead was changed from previous issues to read: "Information Exchange Among Libertarian Nomads and Troglodytes." Tom explained this change in an article on page 2:

INTRODUCING LIBERTARIAN TROGLODYSM

As the masthead says, P-I is now for nomads AND TROGLODYTES. "Troglodyte" or "trog" means, to us, someone achieving freedom through underground concealment. P-I has broadened because mobile and subterranean lifestyles intergrade well, and because nomads and trogs can have much to trade.

Libertarian troglodysm today seems to be where nomadism was a few years ago: much talk − some of it far out, but not much action. But I believe many will develop underground facilities; at first to supplement, then to partially replace nomadic life forms.

I adopted motorized nomadism as an excellent INTERIM life form, especially suitable as the first major step out. Motorized nomadism offers a high degree of freedom with economy and ease of accomplishment, and provides a good environment for eliminating hang-ups and gaining libertarian skills. But even when choosing it, I was well aware of a serious shortcoming: the dependence on State-controlled highways and fuel. And I planned to eventually eliminate this compromise.

Now Roberta and I are ready for more total liberation. This will probably involve a combination of pedestrian nomadism and troglodysm. Soon, we will build a hidden chamber beneath "public" land for storage and emergency shelter. This will be expandable in stages to a self-contained home and workshop. For flexibility, our first shelter at least will be constructed of prefabricated sections, bolted together; our final facility may not be in the same location. (Digging holes is relatively easy.)

To most people still in little boxes (city apartments, etc.), I continue to recommend motorized nomadism as a first stage in liberation. At this time, troglodysm is more difficult and demanding. It requires greater investment (in time if not money), more skills (there are no new-and-used cavern dealers), and a more complete break from the Servile Society. Any mistakes are more costly. Finally, planning which gets big and grandiose usually becomes a substitute for, rather than a prelude to action. It's better to actually achieve personal freedom in small steps than to only dream of utopias.

In future issues, we will tell more about our shelter, our anticipated lifestyle, and our reasons for choosing pedestrian-nomadic troglodysm over yachts, new country developments, and other high liberation forms. TOM (PREFORM #8, March 1970, p. 12).

In PREFORM #9, Tom relates what happened the first time they set out to dig an underground den:

Here is a report on our happenings and plans. About 10 days ago, we were surprised by four bludgies – 3 forest rangers and a Ventura County deputy sheriff – while excavating our first (attempted) shelter in Los Padres forest.

The day before, it seems, while we were away, our area was intensively searched for a lost boy. The bludiges discovered our camper, parked deep in the woods. They also noticed we had camouflaged our trails, which further aroused their curiosity. They did not (then) discover our shelter site, 200 yards away, which was covered and adequately concealed.

(Bludgy – rhymes with pudgy – is short for bludgeoner, was coined by Roberta, who doesn't believe that the name of a useful, inoffensive animal (pig) should be an appellation for usually offensive beasts.)

The next morning, the bludgies came again to the camper. We were both away from it, but, unfortunately, our digging sounds – hammer on digging bar – were audible; we were not yet far underground and so were working with the hatch cover off.

When asked, I explained that the hole was for mineral exploration. (As it turns out, one can't file a claim until one finds minerals of value.) But with our well-crafted entrance way in place, complete with electric wires, vent pipes, and a hatch cover festooned with a bush and surface debris, they didn't believe me.

When asked about our concealed trails, I said something like, "Never know what people will come wandering through the forest. If they find camper tracks, they will follow them. And my wife might be at the camper alone..." To this, one of the bludiges replied, sardonically, "Yeah, never know what kind of people you will meet in the forest."

Had they arrested us, apparently the only charges they could have made were for camping outside of authorized campgrounds and cutting a few tree branches. Our hole was apparently not illegal.

This brings up an interesting question: Why didn't they arrest us? Certainly our behavior was "suspicious." If it had been up to the deputy sheriff – an extremely uptight, paranoid type – I suspect we would have been busted – for further investigation if nothing else. But the forest fuzz were not eager to press charges. Of course, we were not doing anything especially heinous in their eyes (our campsite was neat and clean – no trash strewn around, no campfire remains, etc.). Also, perhaps, they guessed part of the truth about our hole and were semi-sympathetic. But the main reason, Ii believe, is their own vulnerability. They really can't control "their" forest and some of them realize it. Their installations and equipment are often "vandalized" even now. And the more they hassle "the public" for inconsequential infractions of their rules, the more "vandalism" they must expect. (It wouldn't be difficult to destroy one of their $50,000 helicopters, for example.)

We returned to our site two days later and salvaged our entrance way. So our only losses were in time – about three weeks total spent scouting, preparing the squat-spot and digging...

We learned from our experience. We are improving our techniques; gaining competence and confidence. Next time, we won't be such easy prey...

So, what have we learned? Our loss was directly due to an unlikely coincidence. Had the search happened two weeks earlier, we wouldn't have been around; had it happened two weeks later, we would have been working with cover in place and warning devices operational, and with camper moved out of the area. But also, in hindsight, we can identify some mistakes:

We failed to check the area for strange footprints upon our return. We used two-phase resin paint which requires a week of heat treatment. This caused us to bring the camper to a squat-spot close to the site. Also, the entrance way was too heavy to pack a long distance. Originally, we had planned to squat a mile or more from our shelter site.

We should have dug with cover in place as soon as our entrance way was installed, even though this cramped our working.

We should have spent more time (away from site) designing/building a lighter, more quickly installable entrance way.

But, this incident has also prompted a searching re-evaluation of motorized nomadism in general. This is the first time in my 2 ½ years of living aboard that I have been hassled while parked in a well-prepared squat-spot. While vehicle squat-spots are relatively secure (compared, at least, to conventional living accommodations), they are not so safe that we feel fully free. If I hadn't had a driver's license, we probably would have been busted. (If you have to get a permit from the Man "to be free," you ain't free.)

With trail concealment, perimeter barricades (extra dead bushes, etc.) and camouflage, we may be close to the point-of-diminishing-returns for vehicle squat-spots. There are more things we can do, but the increased security may not be in proportion to the increased time. (Scouting and preparing the squat-spot at which we were hassled cost nearly a week's labor by both of us.) Basically a four-wheeled motor vehicle with its access trails is difficult to hide.

A pedestrian nomad has it much easier. His tent might be as large as a vehicle, but it can be in a much more inaccessible site.

Of course, our camper is quite secure in a more remote area, such as central British Columbia. But trade (import-export with the Servile Society) becomes more difficult. And, by not relying too much on remoteness for protection, we grow stronger – more capable of coping with threats of coercion – more self-confidently free. (If we rely on remoteness now, what will we do, if in 40 or 50 years, the most remote places on Earth have population densities comparable to southern California forests today?)) And even if a motor vehicle is reliably hidden, one's mobility – the main reason for having the vehicle – is compromised by its dependence on State-controlled highways and fuel.

So we now look upon a live aboard motor vehicle as an often desirable ACCESSORY for import-export. And we will maintain our camper indefinitely for this purpose. But motorized nomadism, in itself, doesn't offer sufficient freedom. So for further liberation we will combine troglodysm and pedestrian nomadism.

As a result of the harassment we are accelerating subterranean development. We will now bypass our Phase 1 – a den in southern California for storage and emergency shelter only – and begin work on a home/workshop.

While there is plenty of unoccupied land in southern California, most of it is rather dry. And hydroelectric power seems desirable for underground living. (Combustion, especially of wood, gives off fumes and requires hauling fuel; solar cells or windmill might be spotted.) We presently favor northern California or southeastern Oregon for our home base. British Columbia is a strong second choice.

We have brainstormed and critiqued dozens of different subterranean construction methods. We have rejected the "impregnable fortress" – i.e. any very expensive technologically-elaborate approach. We prefer a relatively simply low-cost facility which can be abandoned if necessary. We believe that increasing equipment beyond a relatively low level will not pay off commensurately in comfort and safety. For one thing, even if a facility is PHYSICALLY undetectable, there is chance of discovery through apprehension and interrogation of people, if people come and go. (In Robert Mirvish's novel, THE LAST CAPITALIST, Dmitri moved their cache any time one of the group failed to return on schedule.) Increasing the group size would reduce per-person cost but would also increase people-related risks.

Some of our ground rules are: Any non-native materials must either be expendable (very low cost) or mobile. All valuable equipment must be backpackable with some disassembly. Any technology we develop must utilize mostly native materials. (While we are willing to import finished products from the Servile Society (our camper, for instance), we don't wish to invest time in developing techniques dependent on materials from that society.)

We have rejected a prefabricated design because of weight and technological dependence. We now envision a tunnel in hard soil or soft rock, dug with hand tools and timbered with cut trees. The entrance will be a vertical shaft.

Since we are giving priority to be the troglodytic phase of our future lifestyle, we won't have much to say about pedestrian nomadism for some time. But I don't believe that foot mobility limits one to "primitive" living conditions. The more sophisticated the technology, the less the weight and space required for given facilities. Consider some of the possibilities with lightweight thermal materials, compact batteries, efficient fluorescent lamps, solar cooking stove made out of inexpensive plastic compound lens, microfilm library, etc.

We will head north about June 5 for scouting, then building. If you are summering in the area, I hope we can meet. TOM (PREFORM #9, May 1970, pp. 10-12)

Tom & Roberta responded to their hostile encounter in Ventura County by moving north. In the next issue of PREFORM, #10 dated August 1970, they announced a change of address from a PO Box in Glendale, California to a PO Box in Grants Pass, Oregon. Their announcement said that mail for "Preform, Roberta, Tom, Marshall, and Becker" should go to this new address. From this, I deduce that Roberta's lasts name was probably Becker. This is the only place that was ever mentioned.

In an ad in this issue, Tom expressed a desire to contact others in the Siskiyou area:

"We wish to contact any libertarians living in Siskiyou region – especially Medford, Ashland, Grants Pass, Cave Junction areas. Need not be liberationists but should be open to free-market trade, not just discussion. (For example, if we don't find a secure camper squat-spot handy to our den, we would like to rent parking space on secluded private land.) Must be explicitly anti-state coercion and against The Monster; philosophic fine-points, semantics, lifestyle, hair length, etc. unimportant." (PREFORM #10, August 1970, p. 1)

Tom describes his living situation at that time:

"We are still living in our house-car while preparing a campsite plus various stashes and caches. Our camp – and den soon to follow – is in forest, near a rushing sparkling creek, among high and rugged mountains. (On at least one peak a snowfield has lasted all summer – a natural refrigerator.) It has taken us almost two months of full-time exploring to locate a choice site; several times we became discouraged and almost headed elsewhere. But we persisted and are now happy we did. We will describe our new lifestyle in a future issue. TOM" (PREFORM #10, August 1970, p. 1)

In the November 1970 issue of PREFORM, Tom describes further progress along the same lines:

Our present lifestyle is betwixt and between. Our tent – a big marine-surplus nylon hex-tent, tepee-shaped, was airy and cozy until a month ago. Now, with rain almost every day, often all day, the contents, clothes, books, papers, tools, etc., are continually damp and getting wetter.

But this is the best time of year for trogging: very few people around the back country and ground easy to work, yet not bitterly cold.

So we have two homes at present. I live in the tent back in the wilderness, building our den, while Roberta stays in the camper on some private forested land (swapping wood-cutting for rent) and takes care of other jobs. I come out on our motorbike and hiking, every few weeks, for special supplies, food variety, hot shower, and very nice company (R&R?).

I hope to have the basic structure done by January 1, then we head south for more things from storage, library research, relaxation, and (I hope) much rapping with interesting people along the way, including some we missed on previous trips.

Changing from vehicle-nomad to trog-plus-foot-nomad is proving to be a much bigger transition than was the move from urban apartment to vehicle. This we expected.

We hope to improve communication – of various kinds – once we are established in our new lifestyle. For now, shelter and food must take priority. TOM (PREFORM #11, November 1970, p. 7)

1971:

"We plan to head south in a week or two. Expect to be back up during March and maybe April but busy on den and difficult to communicate with." (from January 1971 letter in VONU BOOK 2, p. 5. Letter continues with same text as next item.)

As van nomads, our lifestyle more or less reached a peak of refinement about a year ago. For a description of a very similar lifestyle, see "Further Report from a Nomad" in the final issue of INNOVATOR.

Now our living patterns are in transition. If you came to Grants Pass now (early January) we would probably meet you there, parking our camper in the back yard of a friend. We can sleep two extra without severe crowding. The seats in the dinette make up into an extra double bed.

Our main activities at the moment are catching up on mail, shopping, and camper maintenance, so I don't think "observations" would be representative.

(While putting out this issue of PREFORM, we are in southern California with our camper in a sunny and pretty, but cool (elevation 5000 feet) squat-spot in the Tehachapi Mountains near Frazier Park. We began this typically-untypical day by making love. Had milk (from dry powder) for breakfast. Dinner was a big pot of brown rice, cooked with some onion and a little meat by Roberta, plus raw alfalfa sprouts. At the moment (early evening, we are munching sunflower seeds. All our food today was from stored supplies except for the onions and meat which were purchased locally. Since getting up, we have been writing/typing PREFORM all day, except for a brief recess when Roberta made bubbles, pretty gliding along in the wind with the sun effervescing off of them.)

Our camper seems most luxurious after living in a tent while working on our den; my first experience living "outdoors" for an extended period in cold/wet country in winter. Much reading of survival books plus summer outings had not adequately prepared me, I discovered. I'll tell more about this experience in a future issue. TOM (PREFORM #12, March 1971, p. 8)

Wood Stoves: After trying about everything I could think of to heat my various mobile shelters, I found the solution in the good old wood stove. The pressure and wick kerosene burners, the catalytic heaters, L.P. gas – they all have drawbacks for the full-time "out backer" or penny pincher. With a wood stove, wherever you go, the fuel will probably be laying around waiting for you. A good armload will keep you snug all day and a little coal or hardwood will get you through the night. Even if daytime smoke will give away where you are, you can always stoke up after dark.

I designed and built a wood stove out of two square 5-gallon steel cans plus about $2 worth of 3-inch stovepipe, fittings, and assorted hardware. Took me one day. Weighs less than 10 pounds. I have used it for cooking at our tent. It is fairly adequate though there are a couple of other things I would do differently if I made another.

Boiling is fast and easy. I cut a hole in the top so most of the pot sets down in the stove. Other kinds of cooking are tricky, requiring constant attention.

It's amazing how warm a little wood kept our not-well-insulated tent, even with 20°F outside. TOM (PREFORM #12, March 1971, p. 10)

On the first page of PREFORM #12, Tom announced that they were changing the printing method and name of their newsletter. PREFORM would become VONU LIFE, and mimeograph would be replaced by photo-offset reproduction. The first issue of VONU LIFE was dated May 1971.

PEN NAMES:

The first page of VONU LIFE #1 included these items:

"Thanks to Roberta and Tom of Preform for much advice and assistance on this first issue, and to all who have sent materials. RAYO"

"To Readers: As part of our lifestyle experimentation, we will live during the next year secluded in a remote wilderness area.

El Rayo, Dr. Gatherer, and Mike Freeman, themselves van nomads and long-time associates, have kindly consented to manage VONU LIFE during this period." ROBERTA and TOM

Clearly, this is meant to imply that Tom & Roberta, and Rayo & Dr. Gatherer, are 2 separate couples, 4 persons. This Mike Freeman, who is also listed as publisher of VL, is not otherwise known to me. The name appears to be an alias. He may have been an actual person who didn't want his real name used, or just another of Tom's pen names. In addition, someone was writing in PREFORM under the name Haelen Hygeia, using the Grants Pass PO Box. And I was corresponding with "Orion," who was picking up Tom's mail from the PO Box. I didn't suspect that these different names were mostly aliases, and I drove to Oregon expecting to find a group of 5 or 6 people. Instead I found there were only 3 people, plus several different pen names used by Tom & Roberta.

After my visit, Tom wrote about me in VONU LIFE #5, p. 1:

"WARM BODIES: One visitor came expecting to count a large number of them & was disappointed because he couldn't."

So, he makes it sound like the fault was my unrealistic expectations, when in fact, the problem was his deliberate deception. And I wasn't expecting to find a large number, as he exaggerates, but maybe 5 or 6.

MY VISIT TO VONU-LAND IN FALL 1971, By: Jim Stumm

Now & then people ask me what happened when I visited Tom & Roberta in Oregon in 1971. Twice I've written an account of my visit in private letters. But I've been reluctant to tell the story in print in the past for reasons that have mostly faded away by now. So the time has come to tell all.

I was corresponding with R.L. Gifford during 1971. He wrote in LC & VL using the pen name of Orion. Gifford was living in Oregon, camping out at "Jack's place," in contact with Tom & Roberta, having been hired by them to pick up their mail from their P.O. box in Grant's Pass. G was encouraging me to come out, painting a rosy picture of an embryonic vonuist community there with great potential for growth. I was ready to make a change anyway & in Sept 71, after quitting my bank job in Buffalo, I drove to Oregon, intending to stay. The final push that led me to make my move at that time was Nixon imposing wage & price controls on 15 Aug 71. In my apocalyptic state of mind at that time, I decided that that foreshadowed the beginning of the end politically, & it was time for me to go underground. What better place to do it than with Tom in Oregon.

My car was a little 1967 Toyota 4-door that I had modified by taking out the back of the back seat & installing a board so I cd [could] sleep in back with my feet sticking into the trunk. Even so, my body just barely fit. I drove out from Buffalo to Oregon in 4 days (& back in 5), driving alone, up to 700 miles a day, sleeping every night in my car. G had sent me directions to a "squat spot" outside Grants Pass where I was to meet him (the spot designated "Grants Pass NE7" described in VL2 p.8). I found it at dusk on the 4th day of my trip & settled down there for the night.

Next day I went into Grants Pass to announce my arrival. I wrote a postcard addressed to the Vonu P.O. Box & dropped it in a mailbox. Then I went looking for the GP mail-drop, which I found easily: a 5 gallon Olympic paint can in a pile of rubbish behind a garage on an alley at a certain address. I left a 2nd message in the drop & returned to my squat spot to await contact (feeling deliciously conspiratorial, as you can imagine). G showed up later that afternoon, having picked up my message in the drop. We drove to "Jack's place" in my car. (G had no car, rode a bicycle.)

As soon as I began to learn details about the situation there, I began to find it much less attractive than I had imagined it would be. In his letters, G had tended to exaggerate, in his youthful enthusiasm (he was about 20 then; I was 27). E.g. Jack's place: In his letters G told me this guy Jack, who lived in California, had bought some land way back in the woods in Oregon, near Grants Pass, & was building a house there. G was camping out there, at the half-finished house, doing some painting or something for Jack, who wasn't in residence while I was there. Before driving out, I had it in my mind that I might camp out at Jack's place for a while, maybe even until Spring, until I became familiar with the area.

Upon arrival at Jack's place, I found it very different from what I had imagined. I suppose it looked like "way back in the woods" to G, a city boy from New Jersey, but not to me. I'm a city boy myself, but I have spent a lot of time in the Adirondack Mtns of NY State, once hiking alone for 3 days w/o seeing another human being. Jack's place looked to me like outer suburbs, thin 2nd growth woods. Apparently Jack had purchased about 5 acres from some farmer & the access road that dead-ended at Jack's house passed right by the farmer's front porch, which was maybe ¼ mile from Jack's house. So the farmer had full view of all comings & goings. It wasn't at all the secluded place I was looking for.

I told G that I would like to meet Rayo & he went off to make arrangements while I set up camp up the hill from Jack's house. I was using a small canvas pup-tent & a thin rectangular sleeping bag. I had a good one-burner gasoline stove for cooking, but I hadn't yet discovered the quick way to light it on a cold morning. My camping gear was inadequate for cold weather camping, & the nights were already starting to get cold.

That evening, as G & I sat around a campfire eating popcorn, G told me that a meeting with Rayo was set for the next day (Sunday). We would be driven to where Rayo was staying by a guy in the real estate business who was a friend of Rayo's. Then, so I wouldn't be surprised & confused, G went on to tell me what I hadn't known before then, that Rayo & Tom were one & the same person. (I was going to meet "Rayo" & the real estate guy always called him Tom.) That meant Rayo's "freemate" (wife) "Dr. Naomi Gatherer" was Roberta. I also learned then that Roberta sometimes used the pen name Haelan Hygeia. So, I had been expecting to find a somewhat loosely associated vonu community consisting of at least 6 people: Gifford, Tom, Roberta, Rayo, Gatherer, & Haelen. Turned out there were 3 people & some pen names. That put G's claims about a vonuist community in a different, less favorable light.

Next day I walked with G across fields & thru woods to the real estate guy's house & he drove us to some rural land he owned where Tom was staying. He drove by a round-about route it seemed, so I wouldn't learn the way. Very James Bond-ish, but wasted on me; I wasn't making mental notes. I believe this was a place where Tom stored stuff in 5-gallon cans stashed in the woods, & he was there temporarily, sorting thru his stuff. It was a nice meadow, near woods, with a stream down the hill, & a long view off down a valley. No houses in sight. Dead end dirt road led to the meadow. We spent the afternoon sitting in a circle near Tom's camper, on overturned 5-gallon cans, munching on walnuts & talking. I've forgotten what we talked about.

My overall impression of Tom was favorable. He appeared 40-ish, skinny, but tough, Gandhi-eske (Gandhi-esque) looking. Strong-willed, kind of a suspicious guy; no one wd [would] call him warm & friendly, but cd [could] rely on him to fulfill any contract or promise he had made. But I knew most of that from his writing. He was, however, something less than the libertarian hero I had built him up to be in my mind. And I was beginning to have doubts about his vonu strategy. For one thing, he was dead set against owning land, but here he was using land owned by someone else to store his supplies, depending on favors from his friends to make up deficiencies in his own program, it seemed to me.

Roberta was a big, strong woman; overweight, tho not grossly fat, & hairy; kind of masculine. I went along with her when she went down a trail thru the woods to get water from the stream. She filled 2 5-gallon jerrycans, must have weighed at least 40 pounds each. I wondered to myself: now how is she going to get those up the hill to the camper? I decided I would make myself useful & carry one of them for her. But before I could make a move, she suddenly grabbed them by the handles on top, picking up both, one in each hand, & marching off up the trail. I stood staring after her as she disappeared around a bend in the trail, astonished at this feat of strength that I don't think I could have managed. It was just her normal daily routine, I gather.

Before dark, G & I returned to Jack's house. Next day I took my car into Grant's Pass to have the blown muffler replaced. (It had blown in the Midwest where Toyota dealers were then as scarce as fish feathers. So I drove it, noisy as it was, out to Oregon.) That afternoon, or maybe it was the next day, Tom & Roberta drove the camper over to Jack's place. As they drove in, they had a small accident that made a big impression on me. The camper had a glass door on the back, like a patio door. They carried a small trail bike outside, strapped on the back. As Tom drove up the washboard road, the camper started bouncing. Before he could get it to stop, the trail bike had slammed against the glass back of the camper a couples times & cracked it. When that happened, the thought occurred to me that now Tom will have to go back into that society to get a replacement for the glass. And it struck me as more than an isolated problem. It was also an exemplar of a fundamental defect of his vonu strategy; He claimed to be free of that society in some sense. And yet at any moment an unexpected event like this might require him to go back into that society for repairs or spare parts, if he wasn't to suffer a decline in his way of living. He depended on that society utterly for equipment in general & for most of what he consumed. He was living on the fringe of that society rather than actually out of it. And only the sufferance of govt allowed him to get away with it. A more authoritarian govt could have snared him easily, e.g. simply by putting up roadblocks & questioning everyone who came thru: Where do you live? Where do you work? Etc. From that moment, the vonu idea seemed a whole lot less effective than I had believed.

But to this day I remain convinced that camper-nomadism is a way to live in reasonable comfort inexpensively, say on $2000/year or less today. So, living that way would give you a lot of freedom, not from the State, but from obnoxious employers. Such a low income would also free you from paying income tax & reduce what you pay in sales tax. And if you spend a lot of time out of sight in the wilderness, you can ignore a lot of annoying regulations. But it will not make you invulnerable to coercion. That overstates it. And if you get rid of the camper & move into a tent to increase freedom by getting off the roads & doing away with need for driver's license & vehicle registration, that would reduce your comfort levels below what I would find acceptable on a permanent basis.

Another thing I noticed was that Tom & Roberta seemed to form a tight, closed society between the 2 of them, with not much need for outsiders, hard for any 3rd person to get close to them (more so than other married couples I have known). G was less close to them than he had led me to believe, not Tom's right hand man, as I had gathered. And it seemed like G cd [could] flit off to anywhere at any moment. He did, in fact, leave for New Jersey a few weeks later, & he never returned to Oregon, although my leaving may have influenced him in that. I saw no evidence that any other persons were likely to join the vonu "community." So where did that leave me, I wondered. Pretty much on my own, if I stayed in Oregon. And I had to do something fast. It was almost October, winter coming, nights were already cold, & I could see that my camping gear wasn't adequate for winter camping. That would have been an easily solved problem, I had money (cash, travelers checks, & a stash of gold coins wired up under the front seat of my car), but it was one more thing to deal with. I had to get settled into some place for the winter, not Jack's place which I didn't like, or if I was going to leave, I had to get over the mountains to the east before snow started falling in the high passes. So I had to decide.

Overall, finally, Tom & Roberta struck me as quite nice people, like a friendly rural couple, a little shabby looking, the sort you'd fine on a remote homestead somewhere & be happy to have for neighbors. But I had been expecting much more. They fell far short of the super-human, libertarian heroes I was expecting. There didn't really seem to be any room for me in their little community, us against the world. It wasn't likely anyone else would join us & G would probably leave. So I decided I might as well go back east. If I was going to be pretty much alone anyway, I might as well make my base on familiar territory, where I had relatives & some other friends I could possibly call on if needed.

I had pretty much made that decision before that evening when the 4 of us spent some time sitting around the table in the camper. We spoke in general terms as if we were going to be staying near each other for a while. I didn't want to say that I had decided to leave. I didn't actually say that I was planning to stay either, although I let that impression stand. I didn't commit myself to anything in particular & no one pressed me to say what my plans were. I don't know what I would have said if they did. I felt I was being a little deceptive & that made me feel uncomfortable, but I was loath to get into an argument with Tom by mentioning the shortcomings I saw in his vonu ideas. I still had a high regard for Tom and I was somewhat intimidated by him even though he was not quite the hero I had thought he was, & I knew this evening would probably be the last time I ever saw him. I didn't want to end up in bickering disagreement. So we had a friendly talk, & I was careful not to promise anything that I wasn't about to fulfill. Later, in the dark, I went back up the hill to my tent.

Next morning, early, I packed up & left to drive back east without saying goodbye to anyone. I left a brief note at my campsite saying I was leaving. Later I wrote to Tom & expressed my doubts about the vonu strategy in writing.

My leaving was partly a failure of nerve on my part, but it was also a reasonable practical decision. What I found was quite different from my expectations, partly because my expectations were unrealistic, partly because I was misinformed by G. I was under pressure to do something fast because winter was roaring down on me. It would have been different if I had come out earlier in the year, in early summer. Then I could have hung around, camping out here & there in the West, for a few weeks & maybe I would have decided to stay anyway, despite my disillusionment with the vonufolk. But then I would have missed interesting experiences that I had over the next few years in co-ops in Buffalo. It's impossible to know what might have happened if I stayed in the West. The Road Not Taken.

CONTINUED ON NEXT PAGE

MAIL ADDRESS: In November 1971, it was announced in VONU LIFE #4 that their mailing address had been moved from a P.O. Box in Grant's Pass to one in Cave Junction. I presume Cave Junction was closer to Tom's camp in the woods.

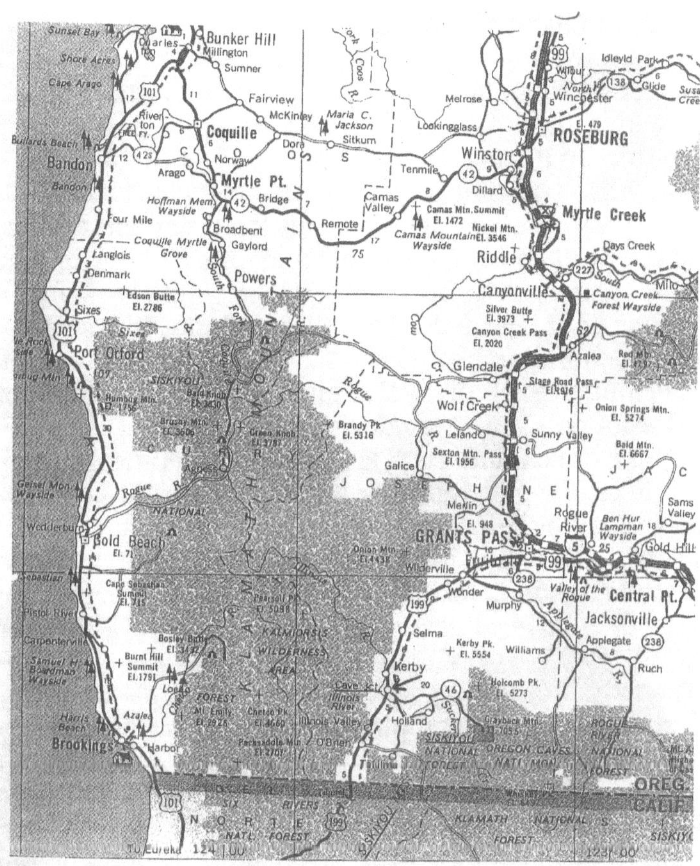

FURTHER REPORT ON SHELTER

Dr. Gatherer and I are living in an A-tent made by placing polyethylene film (20 feet wide) over a rope strung between two trees. Our tent is 9 feet wide, 7 to 8 feet high in the middle, and 35 feet long! This is the first time we have had ample vonu work space sheltered from the rain and snow. One change we have made from our previous A-tents is to leave the ends open, which results in less underside condensation – no drips. We plan to fabricate triangular sections from scavenged cloth which will cover the ends (under the poly) to stop breezes and allow some solar heating. Another change: bracing poles (two pairs) are also placed in an A shape which leaves an unencumbered walkway down the middle. Cost of the poly plus rope was about $15.

Near one end of the A-tent lays our newest creation, in which I lie typing this: we call it a foam hut. It's about 9 feet long by 4 feet wide and 2 feet high, tapering toward the foot end. It is made of 2-

inch polyurethane foam, glued together with a special cement (which may be 3M77, the can which was purchased at Hill's in Grant's Pass, is unlabeled). In one side of the hut is the door, covered by a flap of one-inch foam to which rocks are tied at the bottom to keep it snug. In the other side is a window, covered inside and out with a transparent vinyl-type plastic. (The foam itself would probably pass enough light now, but foam darkens with age.) In the roof at the head end is a screened hole for extra ventilation when our kerosene lamp is lit or in warm weather; a piece of foam plugs the hole when not needed. The foam alone (open cell) provides sufficient ventilation for breathing.

The hut is sort of like a giant sleeping bag except that the domed roof is firm enough to hold position. Under the floor, extending from shoulders to knees when sleeping, is an extra 3 by 4 ½ foot piece of 2 inch foam for comfort and additional insulation.

Based on the few temperature readings so far, the hut provides about 20°F above outside temperature with one person inside, 35° two. This is the body heat alone; when the lamp is burning we must open the door. The coldest morning so far: outside temperature was 20°, inside 57°. We were comfortable nude under 3 blankets.

The foam hut is a big step forward for us in comfort-with-vonu. Until now, when tent camping in winter, we could be comfortable huddled in a sleeping bag doing nothing but reading, on one hand; or doing strenuous physical work, on the other. But how does one typewrite, sew, or repair machinery – work requiring bare hands – in below freezing temperatures? Keeping a stove going for heat means much extra work and less vonu. Incidentally, this issue of VL is the first one typed and pasted up in a tent; until now we have done it in our van.

The foam hut is also a boon for Dr. Gatherer's sprout farm – a tray of glass jars keeping warm with me in the head end. Sprouts grow poorly or not at all during cold weather if just in a tent.

The hut weights about 20 pounds and rolls up into a bulky but backpackable bundle. So far it survived, undamaged, one trip from our van to our base camp. About four 45" by 76" sheets of 2 inch foam went into the construction. Material cost about $50; fabrication (not counting design time) took two days and required two people at times.

We expect to live in our tent and hut full-time this winter except for our brief trip in our van to the Bay area. Our van is presently stashed several miles away; we are still using it for work requiring electricity, which we don't have at camp yet. In the future we expect to use our van mainly for 'import-export' transportation. (from VONU LIFE 4, November 1971; reprinted in VONU book, p. 58)

LETTER FROM RAYO (November 1971)

Your info concerning us being around Grants Pass [G.P.] a great deal is out of date. A couple of times since we moved to Siskiyou we lived in the camper in or near G.P. for several weeks at a stretch. But we haven't done that since last January & don't intend to again.

During periods when I am processing mail (Orion did it during Aug.), I hike & ride on motorbike to G.P. every week to 10 days. This is a fairly long hike/ride totaling about 3 hours one way. During short days of autumn/winter, I barely have time to go, process mail (send out initial copies to new subs on the spot), do half a dozen shopping errands & get back in daylight. If something delays me & I don't start back until dark, the return trip takes about twice as long, since I must go much slower for part of the way. I dislike laying over at G.P. since this means packing along sleeping gear (in cold weather). (I have intended to scout & set-up an overnight camp stash near G.P. but haven't got around to it.)

I now find a visit to G.P. (or any town of that society) to be rather unpleasant – it's the massive impact of values of that society, I think, values I find distasteful. This represents a change for me from a couple years ago when I rather looked forward to occasional visits.

When we do meet people in/near G.P., this tends to misrepresent our lifestyle. Also my visits to G.P. are unscheduled, especially in autumn, winter & spring. I don't relish riding the motorbike in rain & snow. So these are all reasons why we do not wish to meet somebody around G.P.

Now that we are at our winter base-camp, we are better able to meet with people. We will meet them at a vehicle squat-spot which is several miles from our base-camp. The squat-spot is roughly 50 miles from G.P. on all-weather roads (gravel part of the way). The squat-spot is accessible for the average auto in all but the worst weather. The visitor must bring his own shelter. Upon arriving he hikes to a particular tree about a half mile away from the squat-spot which we use as a signal flag pole. He puts a combination of flags on the rope & runs them up to announce his presence. About once a day we climb to a peak near our camp from where we can see the flags with a telescope. One of us (or more, but only one at a time) then go on foot to visit him at the squat-spot. We do not have visitors at our base-camp.

If we should be out of the area for more than a day (unlikely in winter), we leave a message at a guest message drop near the squat-spot. (November 1971 letter in VONU BOOK 2, p. 7)

In another November 1971 letter, Tom proposed an exchange of tape recordings as an alternative to personal visits. He ended with this paragraph:

"Vonuans and applied libertarians talk much about the desirability of technology, and about the pitfalls of "primitivism" and yet still rely on that most primitive means of personal contact – physical visitation. Eventually, I believe, physical visitation will be obsolete for all forms of association except sexual relations and a few personal services." (VONU BOOK 2, November 1971, p. 9)

I commented on this letter and pointed out some good and bad points about tape correspondence. And I concluded:

The point of all this was that Rayo was suggesting a tape correspondence as a substitute for physical visits. He was missing the point about what physical contact is for. It's much more than just a means of communicating specific bits of information. It's clear that Rayo wasn't one for visiting just for the enjoyment of good fellowship, to say nothing of partying. Rayo comment: "Eventually physical visitation will be obsolete..." reveals only his own extreme social isolation and should not be taken seriously as a prediction for a world anything like what presently exists.

Humans are social animals. That's coded into our genetic structure, though rare exceptions might turn up who are content to be hermits (or say they are, though I wonder). One of the failings of Rayo's vonu lifestyle was that it didn't allow for a sufficient development of this social component. I think a person can get along perfectly well without contact with MASSES of other people. But most people need to be part of at least a small group of maybe 10 to 15 people. Rayo's 2-person vonu "society" was much too small.

1972:

VONU WEEK – 1972:

"Live and learn wilderness-vonu living for 6 days in Siskiyou region this summer. We will show you how, help you: scout site; erect shelter; finesse trails; forage wild foods; eat inexpensive wholegrains; cook invisibly; store supplies; cache valuables. 15 hours personal instruction, demonstration, assistance. We furnish: campsite; tent; mosquito bar; ground pad; cooking gear; food (mostly wheat, beans, rice); lamp; saws; books; maps & catalogs from our library. You bring: clothes, bedding, any personal items such as snake-bite kit, camera, binoculars, firearms. Extras we can furnish (extra charge): bedding; local transportation; vehicle parking; help setting up 'permanent' shelter. Your camp-site will be in forested, low mountain area; swimming hole in clear creek less than ½ mile away; moderately secluded – over mile from nearest settlement. We are still learning too. But maybe we can advance you in your quest. One or 2 people, $40; additional people in group, $10 each; additional days, $1 per person. Sorry, no animals. 20% deposit. Say when & how you will arrive at least a month in advance; we'll send directions to the meeting place."

LETTER TO FIRST VONU WEEK PARTICIPANT (April 16, 1972)

Thank you for reservation for Vonu Week & $10 deposit. May 30 or 31 is fine. Please set exact time & day for meeting you, if possible, so that you don't have a long wait. Any time is okay with us, but meeting place will be easier for you to locate in daylight. Since I haven't seen you for several years, please also provide identifying information, such as colors of shirt, pants, vehicle, which can be seen from a distance. (VONU BOOK 2, page 10)

This Vonu Week event went off as planned. A detailed description written by one participant can be found on the Internet at: www.libertyunderattack.com/tom-marshall-innovator.

There was one other Vonu Week event, a father and son, who visited Tom and Roberta during August 1972. And that was all. There were no Vonu Week events in 1973 or later, although Tom did offer to host something like it, since he wrote in March 1973:

VONU WEEK RESULTS:

Two groups of 2 people each came during 1972 – about what we had hoped for – many more & we would not have had time for other things we wished to do.

Both groups lived during their stays in "tents" rigged out of polyethylene film, within fairly secluded (though not especially remote) wooded mountainous areas. With one group we erected the shelter on the 1st day; the other group used a shelter already in place but later put up a small stash "tent." We supplied dry staple foods & Roberta demonstrated many recipes which can be prepared with simple, economical, storable ingredients. We also foraged wild foods with which we are familiar. One group & I cached (buried) a 5-gallon can of simulated valuables. There were many long raps. On days when they were alone they explored the surrounding land, swam, & read.

Some who came were more knowledgeable in some areas than we, which we expected & happily admitted. In general our clients were well satisfied altho we felt that some portions of our program were marginal. One criticism was that Rayo relied too heavily on words with some subjects (psycho drama was suggested as an alternative.) Another was that we did not check-out clients' knowledge of "conventional" "survival" skills such as orienteering.

Our present plans for 1973 are to offer "custom" services on demand – give demonstrations, set up shelters or supply caches, consult in a secluded setting. Our rates are very low for services which do not require travel into that society – we are still rather inexperienced (though we know of no vonuan who is experienced).

Now that we are solving shelter problems we can devote more effort to communication. We have tentative plans to live in a "visitation area" suitable for squatting & backpack camping during one month of summer (most likely early summer) where we can meet people within a day or so without advanced notice.

A SEARCH – OF DR. G AND RAYO

We find wilderness vonu addicting; often delightfully so, sometimes painfully so. Several years ago, when we became van-nomads, that lifestyle seemed to offer the optimum combination of isolation and access. We were not content to spend a week or two in that society if we could spend several weeks out of it. As time passed so did some of our hang-ups and we wanted to be further out and out more of the time. Now, much of the time, we no longer live in our van- we can't get it far enough out. But we still use our van for supply/communication trips into that society. And, more and more, those trips are bummers. No, it's not that society is getting worse – we are not beat up, thrown into jail, nor run out of town wherever we show up. It's just that our tolerance for shit becomes progressively lower – keeping up ID (licenses expire, and need a "residential address"); keeping things on and in our van "legal"; worrying about our personal appearance being too freaky, etc.

I really like E's comment about putting one's body and house on the highway…"The small space occupied largely by those guys with the red lights on their cars…" Of course bludg-land isn't just the pavement, it's all the space visible from and easily accessible from highways, streets and roads – i.e., almost all the houses, shops and farms of that society. (A big advantage of van-nomadism over "conventional" ways is not that the pavements are safer than the rest of bludg-land, but that a nomad spends less time on the pavements and in the rest of bludg-land.)

Several years ago, when I was just a sheep-person with illusions of enlightenment, maintaining serf-tags (ID, etc.) seemed trivial. (When one is waist-deep in sewage, what's another turd more or less.) Now these are the most unvonu parts of our lives and are correspondingly unpleasant.

We have some experience with bicycles and don't think they're an answer. A bike means **more** time in bludg-land per trip – **more** red-lighters and other dangerous drivers whizzing by. As for bikes not needing licenses, that is just a liberty (legal interstice), not a vonu (relative physical invulnerability), and probably a short-lived one. Already tax-hungry bludg in California are proposing state licensing of bikes, just like automobiles. (The fees will supposedly go for maintenance of bikeways – big deal!)

Nor are we interested in total isolation (yet, at least). We believe primitivism would mean less vonu in the long run. (Primitive societies run afoul of bludg-land sooner or later – consistent avoidance of something requires some knowledge of it.) And there are too many capabilities/things we wish to develop which require equipment, materials and knowledge out of the other society – technology our society doesn't have yet. But personal travel isn't necessary for import-export. All that is needed (for now) is a way to get parcels and messages in and out – interfaces with the freighting and communication services of that society.

Avoidance of personal travel into bludg-land is not without costs. We must buy a particular part, new, through Sears catalog instead of picking it up, used, at a swap-meet. Nor can we engage in business which requires face-to-face encounters. But these costs are small compared to the savings, at least for us.

This brings me to the "retired farmer with pickup truck" who Adam proposed hiring. It is one thing to get some stuff hauled around once a year. It is something else to get mail/parcels picked up and delivered every couple of weeks, which is what we would like. The latter service requires somebody who is not only reliable, but closed-mouth and in sympathy since he is apt to be hassled sooner or later. There are such people (we know several) but they are few and far between.

Dr. G. and I would probably be happy to pay $4 per trip ($100 per year) for such a service. For $4, someone in that society cannot afford to go much out of his way to pickup/deliver at our drop. Even though the retired farmer is sympathetic, he is very much in that society, incurs the "high overhead" (psychic even more than financial) there, and will expect to be paid at that society's going rate. Assuming he goes to town every other week anyway, for $4 it might be worth his while to drive 5 miles out of his way to our drop. This severely limits our base location – a desirable wilderness area is not apt to be within a few miles of the relatively few applied-libertarians we could trust to provide such a service. Even if we find such a combination of person and place, suppose he gets sick or moves away: we must move too or pay much higher fees to somebody living further away.

But, if, say, ten vonuan families or groups lived within a 20-mile diameter area, and each would pay $4 for interface service, that's $40. $40 will hire an applied lib, one day every two weeks – pay for his time and 100-miles or more of driving expenses. We and our drops need not be near his home. Such a service is not to replace long-term storage of supplies we know we will use, such as hundreds of pounds of food staples, but for procurement of the unpredictable items and information – a special part for a new device we are developing, a drug to treat a rare disease, a book.

So, Dr. G. and I are seeking other vonuans who (1) have enough mobility to locate in the same area and (2) have interfacing needs similar to our own – i.e., desire fairly frequent parcel carrying to/from the other society, but do not wish to visit that society more often than once a year (if that often).

Our association needn't be a close-togetherness thing. One needn't approve the way the other combs his face. We can have as much or as little internal trade and personal contact as we want.

Dr. G. and I are fairly mobile. At present we can move our base with less than one month's labor. And we are not hung-up on any particular wilderness spot. Nor is "moving" Vonu Life to a new post office box especially difficult. For climate and nuclear-fallout reasons, we probably aren't interested in any area outside the Pacific Northwest (northern California through southwest Alaska) unless it is outside of North America. And we want to be at least 100 miles away from and upwind of the metro areas of Vancouver, Seattle, Portland and San Francisco.

Perhaps we can first come together in Siskiyou region, then when there are more (20? 30? Families), move to the north coast of British Columbia and find an applied-libertarian with a boat instead of a pickup truck. (There are probably more miles of waterways along B.C. coast than there are miles of roads and streets in

California plus Oregon.) Climate and terrain there aren't too different from here — somewhat wetter, only a little colder. More people would be necessary there than here fortnightly interfacing to be economical, since the interfacer would probably travel hundreds of miles.

We are seeking only those with enough vonu-living experience, especially living in relative isolation, to know their own minds. And with savings, or a source of income not requiring physical presence in that society much of the time. If this idea appeals to you, but you are inexperienced, I suggest first trying vonu-living, by yourself, in an area convenient to you.

We already know at least two applied-libertarians in Siskiyou Region who would probably be interested in providing pickup/delivery; the problem is coming up with enough of a market to make it worth their while.

If you think your head is anywhere close to yours, do write. Let us know your experience, present situation and objectives; also thoughts you have about interfacing with that society. This is a long-term project of ours — it probably won't happen in a month or two. So if you first read this many moons from now, chances are we will still be interested if not already coming together. (from VONU LIFE #6, March 1972)

LIFESTYLE DESCRIPTION, April 1972

We are living in a low-mtn area of the Siskiyou region. Winters are long & wet but mild — mostly rain, little snow. Summers are hot & dry, but there are many creeks that flow year round.

Many of our techniques, especially for shelter, are useful only in this climate. They would not be suitable in desert, arctic, or regions of heavy snowfall (including northeast & north central US).

Our present shelter & techniques (as of April 1972), after a year & a half of experimentation & development, is adequate or better from April thru November; marginal from December thru March. When daytime temperatures are below 45° F, which is often the case in winter, we are comfortable lounging in bed, on one hand, or doing strenuous work, on the other, but not when doing light work that requires standing or sitting. Our highest priority right now is further development of shelter, & by next winter we expect to have adequate year-round shelter. However, during Vonu Week, we will demonstrate present, not anticipated, methods, since new approaches invariably have problems that are discovered & corrected only thru experience.

<u>EMPHASIS</u>: We are living almost full-time in the wilderness, not merely surviving until we can return to "civilization." Our objective is not maximum self-sufficiency as such, but maximum vonu (invulnerability to coercion) with comfort. We use whatever mix of "imports" & native materials will yield maximum vonu, given our present skills & numbers.

We admire any "survivalists" who are able to walk naked into the wilderness & obtain all food, shelter, & tools strictly from what they find there. And we are eager to learn from them. But very few, if any, survivalists live that way all the time. Most do it for a couple of weeks & then return to their city abodes.

While most of our tools & supplies still come from that society, we spend little time there – including time spent earning money to buy supplies; much less time than most survivalists. Gradually we are increasing our foraging abilities & reducing our use of imports, but always striving for maximum vonu-with-comfort overall. All our essential imports are storable for a year or more, so in event of some catastrophy [catastrophe], we will have additional time to learn to do without.

<u>ENVIRONMENT</u>: The immediate area is moderately secluded – a mile or more from the nearest settlement. Some land is unowned; some is private but little used. During summer an average of 2 vehicles per day pass thru on a dirt road. And there are a few unofficial picnic spots along this road that are occasionally occupied on weekends. There is little evidence of people away from the road and major creek.

Within one-day hiking distance are many square miles of much more secluded land. In the creeks there is at least one nice swimming hole; many places deep enough to take a bath or cool off. Within a 100-mile radius there are elevations from sea level to over 8000 feet; areas of heavy timber; areas of scrub timber & brush; old mines & placers; rain-forest to semi-desert.

During June thru September the weather is mostly hot & sunny. However, the rare rainy spells can last a week or longer, so anyone not limited by weight might bring a rain suit. There are a few mosquitos in spring, small biting flies spring thru fall, but not in large quantity in most areas. There is poison oak in many places. For summer we like long-sleeved nylon dress shirts – fairly cool, stops most insects, easy to wash & dry, doesn't mildew if left wet.

VONU LIFE CHANGES EDITORS

Lan, a vonuan of considerable experience, is now editor of VONU LIFE. Dr. Gatherer and I are quitting so th at we can devote more time to shelter and food. Last winter, we failed to accomplish many of the things we intended because we didn't have a shelter that was both warm and roomy. (Our lay-foam-hut is warm, but not roomy; our poly tent is roomy, but not warm.) We want better shelter before another winter comes. Also, we intend to forage more, to see if we can economically reduce our dependence on food imports. We intend to write for VONU LIFE occasionally. (VONU LIFE #7, May 1972, p. 1)

LETTER, June or July 1972

I'm more optimistic about crypto-culture (hidden gardening – JS) than I have may have sounded. With intense cultivation – including irrigation, mulching, poly cover in winter – a small patch will produce much food. <u>But</u> we haven't done it yet.

Shelter remains our big concern, as it has been for 2 years. I prefer to be a "systems engineer" & use other people's components. But there is nothing on the market close to adequate (in respect to vonu with comfort & convenience) so I have to develop/build components. But our current approach (plinu) will be completed by Autumn, and if it proves out, we will be shifting major effort to food and communication.

Now that I'm not involved with VONU LIFE (except for an article now & then, & occasional mail pickup & relay) I will try to do better on personal correspondence. Thoughts on this topic:

While newsletter forums (VL, LC) have their uses, correspondence is better for some things. Disagreements are more apt to be resolved when people disagreeing are not verbalizing for an audience. Privacy is greater because info is relayed selectively, friend-to-friend, not broadcast. Correspondence as a whole can be thought of as a vast, decentralized, discriminating communication net.

One thing: I now put destroy-after-reading writings on different sheets of paper than okay-to-keep-and-maybe-pass-on writings.

The fastest way to reach me usually is still VONU LIFE (R). Sometimes G or I pick up; sometimes Lan (or whoever picks up for him) does, in which case it gets left in a drop for us.

I can guess a couple of questions you probably had about Lan so I'll answer:

Trustworthy? While he doesn't have an objectivist/libertarian background, I'm convinced he is vonuan or vonuist. Character references he supplied (upon my request before I parted with VL) were impressive tho not of the "club." I've never met him face-to-face, but I don't consider that important because I'm not good at evaluating people that way. (He may be more than one person for all I know.)

Visitable? So far as I know, not; his private conduct is like his published policy. I've suggested to him that we explore trade possibilities, especially pooling purchases and trips, but so far no response. This rather irks me since, in VL, he was all for local trade with outsiders. Apparently he takes the position that another vonuan who knows he is vonuan is less than to be trusted than a redneck who doesn't know what he is. But we have exchanged letters, books, and publications, through drop. Also I sold some stationary (bulk purchased) along with VL. So maybe more trade will develop.

Despite my irritation, my overall impression is that he is thoughtful & careful ("cool") – that maybe he has been at it a few more years than I have – has thought of a few more angles, has gotten his lifestyle further refined.

He doesn't seem well-informed in economics. Unfortunately the "club" literature he has seen (exchange pubs) apparently have turned him off to "libertarianism." (He categorized it as "political" (collective-movementist?) in his comment to me. We haven't gone into it further.)

I think his main interest in VL is, he thought he could increase circulation & make quite a lot of money. But after seeing his first issue, I'm not so sure. He didn't make the kind of changes I had expected. I have contractual strings on VL – if he loses interest & lets it drop, it comes bouncing back to me. (VONU BOOK 2, p. 17)

EXCERPT FROM SEPTEMBER 19, 1972 LETTER

Our lifestyle this autumn and the first part of winter: We sleep in the lay-foam hut under a small poly tent which is within easy commuting distance of our camper. We cook and eat (except breakfast) and do most other things in camper. During spells of good weather, I go for several days at a time to the plinu on which I am still working...I expect we will move to the plinu in Feb. or March, if structure and drainage prove out. (VONU BOOK 2, p. 20)

Editor's Note: "Plinu" is Tom's coined word meaning a semi-underground den, apparently half below the surface, half above, to be distinguished from his completely underground "smial," another coined word, which he abandoned when it filled with water.

EXCERPT FROM NOVEMBER 21, 1972 LETTER

Actually Roberta & I are not as committed to wilderness vonu (at least to the exclusion of everything else) as we might seem. (We go through a period of doubts/rethink each winter.) If it were not for the nuclear threat we might be trying to build a smial under St. Monica mountains or maybe Tilden Park (Berkeley). At the moment Roberta is more sold on wilderness vonu than I. We now look upon ourselves as "vonu experimentalists." We can afford the luxury of this partly because we AREN'T in a desperate need for vonu – no immediate problems with draft, school-aged children, etc.

The main emphasis of Roberta & I right now is developing a way of living FOR us that combines maximum vonu with comfort. Until we have problems of living the year around better solved than we do at the moment, it is foolish to attract others to join us. (If somebody wants to experiment on their own, fine. Good luck.) Orion's visit the previous summer convinced us that we were not yet prepared for associating (at least on a year-around basis) with anyone who wasn't at least as experienced/equipped as we were. The thing we can do which is most likely to attract others, & attract them on a sound basis, is to increase the vonu/comfort/convenience/capability of our own lifestyle. What people might then come, I have no idea. Most likely they will be people we don't even know of at present. (VONU BOOK 2, p. 21)

Shelter: Shelter development is still our biggest activity. Our situation the past year: vonu, comfort, convenience, winter - we can have any three of the four but not all four at once; i.e., we can live in vonu and comfort with convenience but not in winter. We can be comfortable and vonu during winter if we forgo convenience to do many things. Etc.

We are still living most of the time in polyethylene A-tents; part of the time in our van. Our A-tent survived the winter with one minor mishap. There was an exceptionally heavy snow while we were away. Snow slid down the poly and piled up at the bottom on each side, bowing in the sides and dragging down the ridge rope. The poly was punctured in a few places by sharp-cornered objects under it but didn't tear, nor did the polypropylene ridge rope (1200 pound test) break.

Other problems with the simple A-tent: cold in cold weather; no insect screening of tent as a whole (we use mosquito bar over bed only); no blackout of tent as a whole (again, we use curtain over bed); reflections from sides which slope south, east or west visible for several hundred yards; fastening of sides must be changed whenever weather changes from wet/cool to hot or back (frequently during spring and autumn); clear poly has a short life in daylight.

Our poly tent has held up almost a year now but little direct sunlight strikes it. We tinted it near the ridge with cheap spray paints for possible ultraviolet protection and for better blending with the surroundings. The paint rubs off easily but this isn't a problem so long as the tent doesn't move much. The paint appears much lighter on the poly than on the top of the can so dark shades should be purchased.

Our lay foam-hut has proven very satisfactory for tasks which can be accomplished in a reclining position such as sleeping, reading, eating, erotics. We slept in it from October through May. With two people inside, temperature rise over outside was about 35°F about six inches above the floor. During warm weather the door was left open, covered only with netting. The 2-inch-thick open-cell polyurethane foam (commonly sold for mattresses) "breathed" well. Even on the wettest days the inside stayed dry though beads of moisture condensed (and kept evaporating) on the outside. This was with two of us breathing inside with all vents closed. (The foam hut was inside the poly tent which sheltered it from rain.) At first we laid the foam hut directly on the plastic ground cloth but (apparently) moisture diffusing through the bottom condensed on the plastic and caused puddles in low spots. Then we built a foundation of boughs a few inches above the ground and ground cloth, which solved that problem. No stiffness was noticed inside. A vent plug, about six inches in diameter, was removed from the top when we used a kerosene lamp inside; the lamp was placed under the vent. Ordinary foam is very inflammable so care is required around fire. We replaced the internal brace (to prevent sagging) with cords to overhead runner-ropes which also held up the blackout trap.

The foam sit-hut is not yet satisfactory. Temperature rise was only 15°F over outside (one person); not enough for work requiring bare hands on cold days. Temperature rise was no greater than in lay-hut (also 15° with one person) even though dimensions were smaller – 4 x 6 x 2 feet versus 4 ½ x 9 x 2 feet, probably because there wasn't a tight fitting at the waist. I had hoped that the warmed air, being lighter, would remain trapped within the hut, but apparently there was much convection. Either a snug waist closure or a bottom will be needed for greater warmth. Already it is difficult to get into or out of, and to pull additional things inside. A tight closure or bottom will increase difficulties.

Foam is an easy and "forgiving" material to work with. A piece not quite the right size can be compressed or stretched into place. A mis-cut piece can be glued back together – a join with the proper foam cement is as strong as the foam. Foam is fairly expensive though – our lay hut consumed over $50 worth.

In winter/spring 1971 we built a small den, intending to use it for a workshop and storage. First problem was condensation. In summer warm air trickles in and cools, relative humidity rises past 100%, and dew condenses on everything exposed. Last autumn I put in a fix, I hoped, and left it alone for the winter. I have yet to learn if the condensation problem is solved because last winter it flooded. The den almost filled with water; the things stored in it washed around some and got wet. For drainage there was a four-inch pipe topped by a one-foot cross section of rocks (covered with plastic to keep finer dirt out). This gives an idea of the flow of water! The water apparently welled up from the bottom. The structure was intact except for some washing near the entrance way. I opened up entrances to the drain some more in case clogging was the problem. Next spring I will visit it again and see if the problem is solved.

But, for now anyway, I'm turned off to completely underground structures too big to be assembled away from site (watertight) and packed in – i.e., much larger than a 55-gallon drum. Not only are condensation and drainage likely problems but much equipment is needed to make a den liveable – artificial light and ventilation at least. And the basic structure must be strong to withstand soil pressure/weight. This results in the structure being heavy. This, in turn, requires that the structure be built mostly of native materials – prefabricated sections would be too heavy to backpack very far – no point having a den if there is a conspicuous vehicle trail leading to it. Volume of our den is about 400 cubic feet. Construction time of basic structure was about 400 person-hours. Materials cost less than $100 – mostly plastic film, cord, pins (nails with heads clipped off), drain pipe, and plywood and glue for entrance. Most time consuming was not digging but preparing timbers: scouting trees which could be removed without altering the appearance of the environment, cutting, trimming, transporting, smoothing or debarking, drilling holes for pins. This was all done with hand tools. The only power tools which would have saved significant time would have been a drill/sander.

I now believe our first den was over-designed with respect to vonu, considering the remote and rugged area in which it is located. I would guess the mean time to discovery (MTD) under present conditions as 2000 years. An MTD of 2000 means that if I had 2000 such dens I would expect about one per year to be discovered by somebody.

We are now working on two types of shelter. The first we call a plinu. (That name has no particular significance.) It is semi-underground, like the shuswap but of different form to provide more light and (hopefully) remain dry in wet climate. After the problems with the den, I am proceeding cautiously. I am only building the basic structure this summer and autumn. If that stands up to winter rains, snows and winds, we intend to complete it and move in in early spring – hopefully early enough to check its insulative qualities. The interior will be insulated from outside air but not from the ground, thus using the ground as a heat source during winter and as a heat sink during summer. Ground temperature a few feet down remains about 55°F during the year around in most areas of this region. I expect the inside will remain about 50°F on all but the coldest days. Our objective is to be able to perform all kinds of work in comfort without an artificial heat source. I'm designing for 50 years MTD.

The second type of shelter is an improved poly tent. Unlike the plinu it is for warm weather use only. It is simpler and easier to construct than the plinu.

We have sent inquiries to many manufacturers and dealers in polyethylene, but have yet to find a source of wide (at least 16 feet) plastic in colors other than clear and black, in quantities less than 5000 feet. A source for Monsanto "602", a clear poly but with ultra-violet inhibitor, is A.M. Leonard & Sons Horticultural Tools, Box 816, Piqua, Ohio 45356. Developed for greenhouse use, "602" supposedly lasts two years in direct sunlight compared to six months for ordinary polyethylene. But a 20' by 100' sheet costs $39 plus shipping, compared to $20 to $30 (West Coast) for ordinary clear.

For general storage we are now using wide-mouth steel drums, in the 10 to 17 gallon range, with tops clamped with circumferential bands. With a good gasket these seal water tight. We store food and other supplies which must be kept dry in 4-mil poly bags within the drums. For long storage I place drums under a small open-sided poly A-tent, similar to A-tent previously discussed but with black poly for longer life. Sides are tied out (as with "summer" tent) for ventilation and snow protection. The tent provides extra shade in summer and rain/snow protection in winter which reduces rusting of the drums and saves contents in case both gasket and bag leak (which has happened with one drum in 20). New gaskets would seal better but I haven't found a source.

General thought on shelter: Build small shelters and have several in an area, far enough apart so that discovery of one is not likely to lead to discovery of others. Use soft foot gear, such as moccasins lined with foam, for travel between them and to water source and latrines, to minimize disturbance of ground. (Good conservation and vonu.) Use hard foot gear (regular boots) only when hiking outside of home area. Advantages of multiple small shelters: many more suitable sites; easier to put under/between trees and bushes with little cutting; not as visible; small structure with few possessions appears less 'permanent' if discovered, less likely to arouse curiosity or hostility. Disadvantages: travel between them, items not always at hand when wanted.

Vonu: We have much less contact with unsavory characters now than three years ago when we were living in a van in Southern California. The improvement is due partly to living in a less populated region, partly to our increasing skills. While living at secluded squat-spots, during the last 18 months three groups have seen our van. Two of these, including the only bludg, happened by while we were parked on "private" land with permission. One object, weighing 50 pounds and worth about $15, was stolen from a stash we had on "private" land (with permission). No stranger has seen any of our camps, even though some have been in relatively accessible areas. No one has molested us personally.

Projects for the next year include warning systems and more tell-tale techniques – the latter to indicate if anyone has been near our shelter in our absence.

The bad guys may be trying harder. But we are getting better at hiding much faster than they are getting better at seeking. It's amusing to read letters from people – "conventional" dwellers, mostly – who delight in telling vonuans about all the things Big Brother will do to stop them unless they join a political crusade or something. Big Brother already has 60 million laws and regulations or so. If all laws were consistently enforced, almost every man, woman and child would be in prison for one or more violations. But Big Brother can only extort so much taxes to hire bludg and build spy devices. And taxes are already to – or beyond – the point of diminishing return. Each additional rule to be enforced means existing rules get enforced less.

Someone has worried because the bludg are talking about "requiring" permits to enter "public lands." To put this in proper perspective, consider that for many decades permits have been "required" to hunt – even small game in most states. How many mountain people have ever shot a rabbit or squirrel (at least)? How many had a permit to do so? How many went to jail or were fined for doing so? Of course there are game wardens and every now and then they catch somebody. The few convictions I have heard of were all on circumstantial evidence: somebody's deep freeze was searched and deer meat was found. No doubt the suspect had invited all his friends and relatives to a venison banquet and somebody talked.

Around Siskiyou some freaks are still using 18th-19th-century methods. Someone walks several miles into the woods on "public lands" and builds a conventional cabin out of trees he cuts to clear a garden. And, so far, the bludg do not even have the resources to find and run off these people. Or perhaps the bludg know that if they start hassling a lot of people, some of the least imaginative will start burning the woods. And that would make many people unhappy including the bludg's superiors – the bureaucracies obtain a large part of their funds by selling timber to lumber and paper companies.

We should not get cocky and careless, of course. I appreciate specific, detailed information on tactics and devices in use or readily available, along with suggestions on how to foil these. I have no use for vague, hysterical warnings. Ways of "fighting back" should be considered. But nothing so foolish as shooting at every bludg one sees, or joining political movements. There are several thousand years of evidence that this kind of "fighting back" only makes matters worse.

Regarding Paul D's concern about super metal-detectors: Rocks do move, around here at least. Not every rock every day, of course. But they get pried out by roots, turned over by bears, washed down hillsides, knocked over by other rocks, etc. About bears: while they can be fantastically destructive they create excellent diversions. One bear in one day will alter the landscape more than will a vonuan in a year, if the vonuan is halfway careful. To obtain food a bear turns over rocks, digs after little ground animals, and breaks down branches on berry bushes. Anyone seriously looking for squatters would need a crew of men and a helicopter, full time, to check out the work of each bear. Or else they must exterminate all bears. Then there are deer, porcupines, pack rats.

Of course, bears don't build fires or use metal drums. So woodsvonuans may eventually have to keep fire and metal under cover, stop using them, or create diversions. Anyone really worried about super metal-detectors can always gather up a few dozen empty cans at a dump and leave them here and there, preferably under trees and bushes in rugged country where a helicopter can't land; also leave a few hanging from trees in such a manner that they will bang together now and then for the benefit of detectors which detect the sound of metal against metal. In one day one person could scatter enough cans to keep a crew with "super metal-detectors" busy for at least a year.

Of course, wilderness-vonu may not be as easy here as it apparently is in "totalitarian" Russia where whole factories are hidden in ravines.

Anyone know of a source for an inexpensive nuclear-war detector? This is most likely a special AM radio receiver which sounds an alarm if most broadcast stations shut down or change frequency. It could be made by interfacing an alarm with the automatic gain control circuit of a radio, but there might be time-consuming problems so I'd rather buy one. Without such a device we might not learn that a nuclear attack was made until days or weeks later, and ingest radioactive fallout we could have avoided.

Back to bears: IIow can they be repelled from a camp not occupied for two months? We have been using a single strand barbed wire electrified fence. But we have been told this won't stop a bear and so far a bear hasn't come around to test it out. I have thought of saving up urine in bleach jugs, then when leaving, tie these upside down at intervals around the perimeter and adjust the tops for a slow drip. Will urine retain the proper smell for several months? Has anyone tried this?

Power: We cooked on a wood stove made from a five-gallon can when we first moved from a van to a base camp, but we have switched back to propane more and more. Now we only cook with wood on an overnight trip where weight is crucial. We switched back for vonu and convenience. With wood we felt we should restrict cooking to nights and rainy days when smoke would not be visible. But at night fire and any light source should be shielded. Also wood smoke is heavier than air once it cools, flows down hills and along creeks, and can be smelled a long way away. Finally, wood gathering and sawing means more activity near camp and more disturbance of environment.

While propane must be imported, we require little. A five-gallon tank now lasts us 6 months, thanks to techniques Dr. G. has developed. Sprouted wheat and beans are palatable after boiling for a minute or two. For rice or millet, the pot is brought to a boil, and then immersed in blankets or foam to retain heat. One further refinement will be to insulate the sides and top of the pot so that less heat is lost while heating to a boil. And we eat many foods raw.

With maximum use of insulated cooking we might be able to generate enough methane from our own shit to replace propane. Other possibilities: charcoal, generated in large batches in a kiln away from camp; 12 volt electric immersion heater plus insulated pot when we have hydroelectric; solar cooking during summer. I hope to experiment with one or more of these during the next year.

Artificial light we use mostly during winter and autumn – at present a kerosene lamp; during the longer days of spring and summer we go to bed at dusk.

For several years now I have wanted to put in a small hydroelectric system – an impulse turbine or a vane pump (the latter suggested by Skye d'Aureous) driving an automobile alternator. But I've been waiting for a shelter more permanent than an A-tent, since there will be several hundred feet of pipe to lay. Even a small creek will provide enough power for our uses. I would like electricity for a fluorescent light to replace the kerosene lamp, and for some electronic development work. At present we use a small gasoline engine driving an auto generator for battery charging.

Sanitation: I'm dissatisfied with our present shallow latrine system – dig a new hole after each defecation, using the dirt to fill in the old hole – because a large area of ground is eventually disturbed, and because of travel between shelter and latrine. We may experiment with deeper holes plus buckets. Any suggestions?

Food: Our diet has not changed much recently. Most of our nutrients still come from stored staples, especially whole grains, pulses and nuts. From February to August we kept records of stored and purchased foods consumed. Quantities are pounds per person per month. Costs are calculated from most recent bulk prices paid.

Stored staples: wheat 15.8 lbs, 67¢; brown rice 6.9 lbs, 69¢; shelled sunflower seeds 5.8 lbs, $2.27; raisins 4.8 lbs, $1.13; popcorn 4.5 lbs, 52¢; red beans 4.4 lbs, 48¢; walnuts in shells 3.7 lbs, 74¢; millet 1.6 lbs, 32¢; dry milk 1.6 lbs, 69¢; buckwheat 0.8 lbs, 16¢; soybeans 0.8 lbs, 12¢; blackstrap molasses 0.7 lbs, 4¢; sugar 0.6 lbs, 7¢; dry kelp 0.4 lbs, 4¢; alfalfa seed 0.4 lbs, 18¢; dry yeast 0.22 lbs, 16¢; limestone flour 0.19 lbs, 0.3¢; subclover seed 0.18 lbs,

8¢; also vitamin pills and seasonings, estimated 40¢. Total 52.4 lbs costing $8.76 per person per month. We ate generously of sunflower seeds because we had a large stash and didn't know how well they would keep.

Other purchased foods: oranges 6.2 lbs, 75¢; grapefruit 2.8 lbs, 28¢; bananas 3.4 lbs, 35¢; apples 0.3 lbs, 3¢; watermelon 1.3 lbs, 9¢; carrots 0.8 lbs, 9¢; cabbage 0.7 lbs, 8¢; beef 0.8 lbs, 57¢; eggs 5, 14¢; cheese 0.5 lbs, 24¢; canned fish 0.3 lbs, 18¢; buttermilk 0.1 qt, 3¢; ice cream 0.4 lbs, 5¢; margarine 0.3 lbs, 9¢; butter 0.1 lbs, 7¢; oil 0.13 lbs, 5¢; garlic 0.06 lbs, 6¢; pastries 0.2 lbs, 12¢; smorgesborg meals 0.35 meals (1 lb ?) 37¢. Total, $3.63 per person per month. I have listed averages, for comparison, but our actual purchases were irregular. For example, during this 5.6 month period we purchased one 15-pound watermelon and ate it, several days later, all in one day. We purchased meat twice, and each time, consumed it within a few days. Oranges, the most frequent purchase, were bought during five trips, and after each, lasted only for a week or two.

Replacement value of purchased food consumed during this period was $12.39 per person per month. Whereas average expenditure on food, calculated for the entire year, was $22.40 per month. (See next section.) Reasons for differences: stores of staples were increased; trips during the 5.6 month period were few and brief, and included not more than two days in populated areas.

Scavenged foods (from grocery trash bins), guess: fruit 4 pounds; melons one pound; vegetables 3 pounds. We made three big hauls during this period – about a hundred pounds total.

Foraged wild foods, guess: meat, cleaned but including bones, one pound; berries, 0.4 pounds; greens, 0.3 pounds. Many berries were picked and eaten while doing other things.

Dr. Gatherer sprouts alfalfa, sub-clover and buckwheat all year which we eat raw as a salad. Wheat is usually sprouted for a day or two to reduce cooking time and improve flavor and digestibility. Some is eaten raw. For breakfast I usually have sprouted wheat and beans, about 4 to 1, briefly boiled. Dr. G. usually fasts until noon. During the day we have one or more snacks of fruits, nuts, milk, occasionally popcorn. For dinner we have sprouts and any other fresh vegetables as a raw salad, any meat, and a starch food which may be rice, millet, popcorn, or bread home-made out of whole wheat flour we grind ourselves. I often flavor rice or millet with walnuts or sunflower seeds. If there is no meat Dr. G. often makes up a stew out of beans or lentils and kelp plus any cookable fresh vegetables on hand.

The berry we gather and eat most frequently is manzanita (Arctostyphylos) which grows abundantly in many areas near the Pacific Coast, is easy to pick (strip off twigs, separate debris while eating), and is palatable if not delectable thru-out summer. Sometimes we reach areas growing many blackberries, black raspberries or Amelanchier (saskatoon berries) at the right time and in a good season and pick gallons in a few hours. But, except on such occasions, foraged berries are expensive compared to imported fruit, even with our low overhead. On a typical occasion I gathered 9 ounces of red huckleberries (Vaccinnium) in two hours. So, on our infrequent trips to town, Dr. G or I top our load on the return with fresh fruit and vegetables to the maximum weight we can handle.

During the last few months foraged meat has included several mice, one rat, several squirrels, one porcupine, one rattlesnake. The mice and rat were caught in ordinary household-type traps. We began trapping for reasons of self-defense, then decided not to waste the meat. The mice were prepared as Olson's Outdoor Survival Handbook suggests: remove skin and guts, then grind or pound them up, bones and all, into a patty. All rodents taste about the same. Mice are easy to trap in winter and early spring, but not the rest of the year when their food is more plentiful. The porcupine and rattlesnake we just happened upon. The porcupine was impressive until it was cleaned; it seemed to be mostly guts. The liver, though, was big and good tasting. Its muscle meat was tough even after a long boiling. The rattlesnake, killed with a stick, was easy to clean, mild flavored and very bony – time consuming to eat. The only deliberate hunting recently has been done by Dr. G. who obtained squirrels and larger animal. Cleaned weight of small game: porcupine about 3 pounds, most squirrels (grey) over one pound, rattlesnake (two foot) 9 ounces, rat 4 ounces, mouse ½ ounce. Cleaning and pounding up one mouse takes me about 10 minutes, so unless I become more adept, mice are expensive meat.

Nutritionally we prefer small game to deer because we eat it fresh; no preservation problems. We are still using some powdered milk and dried yeast which is probably undesirable for long term good health. In April we resolved to purchase no more meat because of expense, contaminants, staleness and preservation difficulties; so far we have kept to it. On two occasions I went for a period of two months with little animal protein and discovered, toward the end of the period, that I could not do rigorous physical work two days in a row – if I attempted to I felt extremely weak. (I felt okay so long as I worked every other day.) Since I had vitamin and mineral supplements and plenty of calories, I'm inclined to believe I had a marginal protein deficiency. Dr. G. has not experienced this. Our staple diet contains more than recommended minimums of essential amino acids in seeds and nuts. But the human digestive system may not be efficient at digesting protein in the presence of a large amount of carbohydrates (seeds are a mixture). And digestive efficiency varies from person to person.

We have not yet put much effort into trapping; shelter and storage have been consuming most of our time. When we do, probably this autumn, we hope to obtain enough small game to replace dry milk and yeast. Also we will experiment with mini-grow-holes for year-round fresh vegetables.

Finances: Dr. G. and I recorded personal expenditures for a period of one year ending this month. Results: *Food:* $536.42 subtotal, including: dry staples (storable) $365.45; spices and flavorings (storable) $10.65; fresh fruit $48.54; fresh vegetables $11.91; fresh meat, cheese, eggs, fluid milk $58.32; 'junk foods' – store-bought ice cream, cookies, bread, TV dinners, canned foods, candy $17.89; prepared meals (restaurants, visiting friends) $17.86. *Shelter and Storage:* $713.05 subtotal including: materials such as plastic film, foam, rope, cord, drums, nails $452.86; appliances, devices and their parts, including stove, lanterns, pack frame, inverter, traps, etc. $116.34; space rental, mostly for storage $43.24; propane and kerosene for cooking, lighting and occasional heating (van) $21.50; tools $14.61; cleaning and miscellaneous supplies $14.50. *Transportation:* $201.24 subtotal, including: gasoline, including tax $124.06; parts and oil $60.08; licenses and tolls $17.10. *Clothing:* $72.22 subtotal, including: materials thread and needles $26.24; footgear $26.62; other ready-to-wear clothing $9.81; laundromat (when in towns) $9.95. *Communication:* $64.57 subtotal, including: books and magazines $32.67; postage (partly estimated) $15.00; phone calls $10.90; stationary (partly estimated) $6.00. *Other:* $32.82 subtotal including: medical, dental and personal supplies and services $28.95; taxes (federal excise and California state sales tax, not counting gasoline) $0.71; miscellaneous $3.16. *Errors and Unrecorded:* (plus) $3.47. *Total:* $1616.85 for one year for two people.

We were surprised and chagrined at the total – higher than the average for the two previous years. Explanations: We built up stores of staples, shelter material and clothing materials so these figures do not represent one year's consumption. Also many shelter items are (hopefully) durable goods. On the other hand our van and motorcycle are depreciating (but probably won't be replaced). Much of our shelter work is intentionally experimental and therefore scrap-generating so we might consider it a business expense. We are still betwixt and between two lifestyles – van-nomadism and something we are still developing/discovering – which increases costs. Excuses!

Seldom were we consciously stingy. We bought most of the things that we saw or knew of that we wanted, but few things of that society appeal to us anymore. Exceptions: no meat or restaurant meals purchased since April; we bought some new books but passed up others on the supposition we could buy them used, borrow them from friends, or scan at libraries.

We put 4300 miles on a van, including two round trips of 2500 and 800 miles, and about 2000 miles on a motorcycle. Our trips to towns of the area were few and brief but we loaded up on fresh fruits and vegetables when we came back. Most of the junk foods were consumed one several-week stay around large cities – the psychological pressures began to get to us.

Comparing our expenses with those of a traditionalist agrarian family, the Colemans, reported in *Wall Street Journal* and reprinted in The Mother Earth News #11: Per person (counting their two year old daughter as one half): food $268 (us) compared to $200 (them, though they claim to grow 80% of theirs); transportation $101 (us, and we are 'nomads'?!) to $300; tools $7 to $80; shelter (except tools) $350 to $80 (their conventional cabin was completed and land was purchased previously); other $83 to $140. Total, $808 (us) to $800 (them).

While we are interested in developing vonu sources of income, so far we have been more concerned with reducing expenses. If expenses are very low, only a few weeks per year spent in a city will suffice to earn money.

Associations, Attitudes, Objectives: At the moment there are very few vonuans – perhaps several hundred in North America. And these are many different places and different life-styles. Most are not in contact with each other. At times Dr. G and I crave association with more people, not only for economic benefits such as pooling outside purchases and trips but for interaction with different minds. But we have discovered that association with sheep-people or bullshitters only makes us 'lonelier'. Such association is like a drink of salt water to a thirsty man. We much prefer just to be with trees, flowers, birds, brooks – and the few people with whom we share values and goals.

But I don't think this will be a problem for long. More and more people are rejecting the attitudes and roles of the servile society. While only a small minority of the whole population, they number tens of thousands. Some attempt to "turn back the clock" by moving to farms or small towns. But rural dwellers are conspicuously unfree, so those who really want freedom will search in other directions.

A vonuan, to me, is not just someone living in a particular manner. Life-styles may change. A life-style which was vonu 100 years ago may not be vonu today; some life-styles vonu today were not possible 100 years ago and may not be vonu 50 years from now. A vonuan is someone who places a high value on relative invulnerability to coercion – someone for whom freedom is worth a fair amount (though not infinite) of effort, inconvenience, discomfort. To a vonuan, vonu is not just a means to other ends, nor is it an ultimate end – like most qualities of life, and life itself, it is both. A vonuan will choose whatever way of living offers personal sovereignty and will change life-style again and again if necessary.

Although life-style may vary, a vonuan can be identified only by what he does – especially by perseverance over a long period, not by what he says. Words are cheap. This is not to reject ideology. Someone who does not see through the myths of the State will not for long remain vonu, if by good fortune he should become vonu. But anti-state ideology isn't enough.

If freedom were free (more precisely, if vonu were gratis), almost everyone would be free (vonu). But freedom isn't free; it is quite expensive and will likely remain costly in the foreseeable future. Most people presently alive do not value vonu very much. One reason, perhaps, is that during thousands of years of pre-technological agriculture servility had a survival value. During this period conventional farming was the most efficient way of producing food. And it is difficult to conceive of a life-style more subject to coercion than that of the traditional farmer. Not only is he visible and usually separated from his fellow, but "his" home and land are especially vulnerable to attack. Servility was not generally pro-survival prior to agriculture. When North America was "settled," few of the natives, who were mostly hunters/foragers, were successfully enslaved. To obtain obedient subjects the bludg had to bring slaves and indentured servants from the most agrarian societies of West Africa and Europe.

I don't know if servility is due mostly to genetic inheritance, to cultural background or to slave-school training. Most likely it is an interaction of all three. But I don't believe that any amount of "education" (propagandizing) will change the attitudes/values/intelligence of most adults. Nor do I believe that the majority can be manipulated into a "free society" by some elite of would-be philosopher kings. Such an effort will, at most, only change the rulers. So long as most people can be easily manipulated, they will be manipulated for the aggrandizement of the manipulators.

Traditional agriculture is on the way out. (At the moment quite a number of people are playing return-to-ye-olde-homestead games, but few are producing enough food even to feed themselves.) Barring a catastrophe of sufficient magnitude to destroy technology world-wide, I predict that within a few decades there will be inexpensive, light-weight, mostly automated bio-chemical devices capable of converting most organic compounds into most other organic compounds. Load the hopper with dead leaves or sawdust, insert the proper program, wait a few days, and out comes food wafers which are at least as nutritious and tasty as most of the stuff sold in supermarkets today. Insert different programs and out comes various plastics for construction and clothing. Of course this is just one approach. Maybe I will modify my digestive track to convert cellulose to sugar. Maybe I will develop hardier varieties of traditional food plants able to grow wild with little assistance, as well as more palatable varieties of wild plants. For the immediate future maybe mini-grow-holes are the way. In any case, I don't think that farming is the wave of the future.

With the decline of agriculture, servility loses survival value. Improving communication has the same effect – people will no longer need to crowd into cities or be visible anywhere to work and play together. Consider the potentialities of pseudo-random-noise radio transmission – coded transmission detectable only with matching receivers. Even that institution run amok, the contemporary State, has this effect; it is its most gullible and easily-intimidated subjects who are most likely to be killed in its wars. So I think in the long run, people who place a high value on personal/small group sovereignty will become a larger proportion of the human population.

Vonu, while difficult, is easier now than it has been since the neolithic period perhaps as high as one or two percent of the population, through accidents of heredity and environment, have values and abilities sufficient to achieve it. To become vonu we must disentangle ourselves from those who won't or can't achieve it –

reject all "reform-society-as-a-whole" schemes, put aside Utopian dreams of world-wide free societies, and get with ourselves and each other – build our vonuums and vonuist mini-cultures.

Possibly I underestimate the potential of existing humans. Possibly most people do value vonu and can achieve it. If so we are more apt to help them become free by becoming free ourselves and showing the way, rather than by joining political crusades. Political reform/revolution/re-education has been attempted thousands of times in hundreds of situations over hundreds of centuries, but at most changes only faces and slogans. Any sort of political movement becomes a contest at coercion and manipulation. Past crusades failed not because of "impure motives," "betrayal," or "defects in philosophy" (why is it invariably *defects*, not the good elements, which come to predominate?) but because of their very nature. Function determines form, means determine ends. The very programs of the State most detested by present "reformers" are reforms-gone-to-seeds of past crusaders.

Dr. G and I did not choose our way of life primarily because we expect a nuclear war or other apocalypse within a few years. While we have considered possibilities of various catastrophes in our planning, if nuclear weapons had never been invented we would probably be living much the same way – perhaps somewhat closer to large cities. Institutionalized coercion – States – is a long-existing social phenomenon; war is only its most dramatic form of destruction. We are striving to reduce vulnerability to all forms of coercion and maximize all satisfactions.

Dr. G and I would like to contact more people with similar ideas, attitudes and actions. If you are not in the region, we invite letters. If you are in the region, let's arrange joint drops at least, maybe meet occasionally. I think the Loose Open Association (as Lan has named it) is the best community model, at least at first. Any closer involvements should come only as people get to know each other over an extended time.

We are now able to provide someone with a food stash, shelter and equipment adequate (most of the time) from May through October. This would be already set up in an attractive, secluded spot – several miles (at least) from any habitation (including other vonuans) known to us. We can bring supplies and mail occasionally (once a month?) to someone who wants to remain completely out of that society for a while. By next autumn we may be able to provide year-round shelter. Our prices are low, or we will barter for services/products we want. Of course don't come to Siskiyou because a few vonuans are already here; hoped-for relations might not work out. Come only if, like us, you evaluate the region as optimum for you. (from VONU LIFE #9, September 1972)

INTRODUCTION TO PACSCRIPT #1, March 25, 1972
(Editor's Note: PACSCRIPT was a one-issue newsletter edited by Tom, as he explains below. PACSCRIPT #1 was 2 pages long.)

I'm doing PACSCRIPT not because I especially enjoy writing, but, on the contrary, because writing is slow and difficult to me. If I relied entirely on personal letters, I could send brief "We are fine. How are you?" notes. But I wouldn't have time to develop ideas, pass on information, or tell about what we are doing.

The cost of offset printing is low, provided a printer has the proper equipment for the job. At least one printer in Berkeley charges only $2.75 for 100 copies of an 8 ½ by 11 sheet, both sides (not mail order). So, with photo-reduction, we can save money as well as time by printing that information which we wish to share with a number of people – postage savings pay for printing cost. Mottos: Every vonuan a publisher. Those that can write well, write; those that can't, edit.

PACSCRIPT is the 2nd zinet (mini-magazine – word coined by Lan of VL) I've started during the past 5 years. The 1st, PREFORM-INFORM, grew beyond original expectations, changed name to VONULIFE, and now, under management of Lan, seems to be becoming the "Popular Mechanics" of freedom achievers. As it grows, VL becomes more valuable for how-to-do-it info but less useful for making/maintaining contacts.

Unlike some zinets, PACSCRIPT is for vonu achievers who would like to meet in person occasionally as well as communicate by mail. For this reason we are limiting distribution to the Pacific Coast. Also for this reason PACSCRIPT is traded only for information, not sold for money. We are not opposed to money transactions, but we wish to keep PACSCRIPT small and personal.

We welcome information relevant to vonu in any form – written or spoken – letters, newspaper clippings, loan of books or magazines, publication exchange, conversations, introduction to other vonuans, leads to sources, etc. I'll assume I may pass on to PACSCRIPT readers unless you say otherwise.

"Vonu achievers" include not only those who are decreasing their own vulnerability to coercion but individuals who offer services which reduce the vulnerability of others such as mail receiving/forwarding, phone answering, storage, squat spots, garden sites, & free market (no tax, no SS, cash pay) employment. All forms of vonu which can be implemented along the Pacific Coast are of interest to us: troglodysm, vehicle nomadism, smumism, boat living, urban anonymity. Opportunities for mutually-profitable exchange are often greatest between people with different life-styles.

I'll assume that every PACSCRIPT reader also reads VONULIFE & will try not to duplicate information that's in there. On the other hand there is much intentional duplication of what is in VZE publications such as VONULINK. (VONULIFE is now an annual book & is separate from VONULINK.) VZE members trade "pool pages". This means I print extra copies of some pages (but not personal identifying data) which they include in their newsletters, & they do the same for me. (See poolpage b from VONULINK, which is part of this issue, for more info on poolpages.) So some of the material in PACSCRIPT is written, edited & printed by others & does not necessarily represent our views.

I'm sending this issue to: personal friends and acquaintances, some people who subscribed to P-I, people referred to PACSCRIPT by VONULIFE, some people who have published letters in VONULIFE (by forwarding thru VL). Distribution of the next issue will probably begin in early summer (likely deadline June 1).

(Editor's Note: When he says "VONULIFE is now an annual, Tom is referring to VL 1973, the special handbook issue. An issue like that was to be produced every year, but only one such issue was ever published. He calls it a book, but it was printed in newsletter format, with very small print, on acidic newsprint paper, which is now, after many years, becoming very yellow & brittle. – The poolpage b mentioned is the same as VONU LINK page VL11 p. 4, on which Lan explains his complicated idea for splitting VL into a number of "zinets," the details & purpose of which never made any sense to me.)

WHAT ARE WE DOING? By: Tom of Preform, March 25, 1973

I'm sitting in our camper on a street in Berkeley putting this issue together (ie PACSCRIPT #1), tho much of it was written (or printed) previously. I'm doing it now because (1) we have a new mailing address & I want to make it known; (2) there is a low-cost printer in Berkeley; (3) I have some spare time over a weekend. Most future issues will be typed, & sometimes mimeod, in our mountain hideaways.

[Editor's Note: The new address Tom mentions is: ALA, Box 91, Berkeley, CA 94701. I believe this P.O. Box was used by several libertarian groups in Berkeley & that ALA stands for something like Association of Libertarian Activists.]

We are on our annual shopping/visiting trip to the Big Cities. From Berkeley we go south along the coast to Los Angeles; then to Baja (Tom has another tooth which needs a gold crown); then back to LA; then north on highway 5 to Tehachapi Mountains; then north on highway 5 to Siskiyou region. Temporary addresses: until about April 5, c/o General Delivery, Laguna Beach, Calif. (write us there if you wish to contact us while we are in S. Calif.); from about April 5 to April 15, c/o General Delivery, Lebec, Calif. (write us there if you wish to contact us while we are in Tehachapi Mtns, or along highway 5). I suggest putting our permanent address on the envelope as return address in case the letter misses us.

(Report on annual food purchases follows, with out-of-date prices. Tom mentions: brown rice, pink beans, black mission figs, pitted Iraq dates, nutritional yeast, wheat, raisins, powdered milk, honey, & dextrose. They buy their year's supply of food on this annual swing thru the Big Cities. –JS)

We can deliver non-organic brown rice or pink beans to any place on our route for $13.50 & $15.00 per 100-pound sack, respectively...Hulled sunflower seeds do no store well, even in cool CO_2 atmosphere. This year we bought sesame seeds at 36¢/lb for a high-oil supplement/condiment.

At present our overall life-style is a blend of van-nomadism, troglodysm & smumism & is moving toward the latter two. (Troglodysm = living physically underground, smumism = moving between several homes hidden in the wilderness – JS). Except for one smial we are still experimenting with, we will not be building more completely underground structures in the near future. Our present shelter work is mostly with small, well-concealed structures on the surface & partly underground. The shift in our interest is due not only to the problems with underground shelters (especially drainage/condensation) but to growing confidence in & ability at concealment on the surface. While it is conceivable that Big Brother may eventually have surveillance systems capable of identifying almost any human habitation on the surface, I don't think this will be a serious threat during the next 20 to 30 years.

We built the basic structure for a semi-underground home/shop last spring/summer. If it over-winters well we will complete the interior & move in this spring.

Although our shelter problems aren't completely solved, we seem to be close to year-around comfort with a high degree of vonu (perhaps 20 years MTH). (MTH = mean time to harassment, an estimate of degree of invulnerability to coercion – JS) We now believe that outside interfacing, not shelter, will be the most difficult part of vonu living. For this reason we are gravitating toward a smum way of life. (There may be an article on smum in VONULIFE 1973.) (There was; see Smumans, The Super Hobos, in VL73 p. 101 – JS)

We are becoming interested in cryptoculture. (Cryptoculture = hidden gardening – JS). A few years ago I had dreams of growing pot in hidden patches & selling it. (Apparently quite a few people are doing this.) Now we are more interested in growing potatoes, to reduce transport (we presently import 1200 lbs a year) & interfacing needs (there may be food rationing within a few years).

We stress physical concealment as much as we do because we are interested in the growth of an alternate economy, not just in personal retreat/retirement. And I don't believe that free-market enterprise will be profitable, much beyond what is already being done (illegal products/services at very high prices, mostly) until quite a few people have secure shelters. Such non-vonu "alternate" enterprises as food co-ops are likely to escape most taxes/regulations only so long as they remain too few & too small to offer substantial competition to fascist (regulated) businesses. There was a big co-op movement during the early 30's, too; the survivors, today, are as regimented & bureaucratic as General Mills (e.g., C & H Sugar).

I have been accused of being some sort of an ascetic who is "dedicating his life" to advancing vonu. This is true, in a sense, but the implications of self-sacrifice & masochism are utterly false. Once status games & food fetishes are weeded out, "physical comfort" essentially means: having a soft warm bed, a cuddly bed-mate, & nutritious food (within easy reach of the bed on days when it's cold & wet outside). There are also various kinds of intellectual stimulations/desires, but there are many alternate ways to satisfy these, including ways compatible with vonu living; one need not duplicate the specific entertainments of the servile society.

I'm "devoting" most of my life to advancing vonu because I find I can have the most pleasure/satisfaction this way. Not only are most tasks interesting/enjoyable in themselves, but there is an added exhilaration in overall integration – having an over-purpose – in most tasks means as well as ends. This is missed by a "playboy" who flits from ski slope to night club to chess game – each activity unrelated to the others. "Advancing vonu", especially wilderness vonu, is an over-purpose especially suitable for a "rational hedonist" because of the variety of physical & mental activities involved & profusion of satisfactions offered. Many over-purposes, in contrast, involve intense specialization of activity & do not fulfill most emotional capacities, leading to frustration or conflicts. (Examples: trying to become world's tennis champion, earn a billion dollars, discover a cancer cure, become a rock superstar.) (reprinted from PACSCRIPT #1 with some editing & comments)

VONULIFE 1973: Tom wrote 16 articles in this issue that he signed as Rayo & he probably wrote many of the unsigned articles. Roberta wrote the longest article, "Far Out Eating," using her pen name Haelen Hygiea, describing her & Tom's diet. There were some other articles definitely written by others, including 2 that I wrote, one signed by Lysander, the other an unsigned letter. But Tom & Roberta wrote most of VL 73.

One article in VL 73, signed "Rayo," provides details about how Tom & Roberta lived in their camper:

CHOOSING A VAN FOR LIVING ABOARD

During the past five years two of us have lived in a motor vehicle three-quarters of the time and in various tents one-quarter of the time. The following are based on our experience and that of personal acquaintances.

Don't expect high vonu in a van. Have "acceptable" ID. A four-wheeled vehicle needs/makes trails and so is difficult to hide well. We have really tried, yet even in our most secluded squat spots, we get hassled (asked impertinent questions) once every couple of years or so. Nevertheless a camper or van may be ideal for someone in transition out of that society – ours has served us well this way.

Don't plan to travel much unless you have plenty of money. Don't buy a cheap well-worn van to move across the continent in unless you are already a fairly-skilled mechanic. Overall costs per mile of a "one-ton" vehicle will be about double those of a small imported automobile.

Single-piece vehicles (vans and motorhomes) and pickup campers both have their advantages. A van is lighter, sturdier has a lower center of gravity and is less wind resistant. Campers are mass produced and often cost less for the same comforts, may be more flexible, and cheaper to license in some states.

Buy instead of build, unless you are already experienced. The money you save building your own camper or making major changes in a van will be a very low return on your time. The experience gained is not very useful except for building more campers. If you do build, don't expect to achieve the overall quality of a factory-built until your *second* one.

Have at least a one-ton vehicle (at least 9000 lbs GVW); maybe one-and-one-half or two-ton. But check out the idiosyncrasies of the extorters in the states you expect to license and drive in. In many states vehicles over one-ton rating are supposed to stop at weigh stations and have commercial plates.

Have plenty of traction and a very low-speed bottom gear for getting off the road. Four-wheel drive is often desirable though expensive; next best is dual-rear wheels with most of the weight on them. VW microbuses and most three-speed standard transmission vehicles don't have a low enough low gear.

Avoid vehicles much longer than a big car – 20 feet – and trailers if you will go into cities or off the road much. Two small vans are more expensive than one big bus, but handier. Also beware of campers with long low overhang.

Furnishings recommended for living aboard most of the time: good insulation; furnace with exhaust vented to outside (I like a propane floor furnace with pilot for quickness of heat, simplicity and no smoke; a very small and light wood stove would be nice for backup); good ventilation; screens on all openings; cooking stove, probably propane, at least two burners; sink draining to waste-water can which can be removed for emptying; five gallon water with spigot which can be set over sink for use, taken down for filling and when moving; propane lamp (or possibly Alladin kerosene lamp) for main light with 12 volt bulbs for quick light and backup; dual batteries; dual propane tanks; polyurethane foam pad for mattress – light, fairly cheap, doesn't mildew; black-out shades or drapes over all windows; plenty of cabinets, closets, drawers and work surfaces. Ideally most bulky furnishings – cabinets, sinks, tables, etc. – are firmly mounted yet easily removed for use of vehicle for hauling – this I haven't seen in factory builds.

Furnishings not recommended: any appliances such as refrigerator or air conditioner which use 120 volt electricity in quantities too large to be supplied by an inverter; john hard-mounted on the vehicle (if a flush toilet is wanted, get Portapotti or a similar make which is a portable self-contained unit and can be removed for emptying); vehicle-mounted water system (we have one but leave it drained much of the year so we don't have to worry about freeze-up); shower and hot-water heater (again, we have one but find we'd usually rather jump in a creek, even in January, or take a sponge bath than spend a half-hour removing impedimentia from the shower, filling the tank, turning on the heater, etc.); unvented heater (fumes are harmful).

Minimize windows in a van if it will be in a city much. I'd consider a skylight (but not a bubble top unless it was somehow retractable).

Squatting and permission-parking both have their advantages and drawbacks. If squatting, one pays no rent. And one has a greater choice of spots including more secluded locations and so is less frequently hassled. Parking with permission, one spends less time finding spots, and is less likely to have to move when hassled – which can be important if one is in the middle of a major overhaul. Permission parking doesn't offer greater security – bludg insist on access to all trails and bludg usually first ask for ID. "We have permission to park here; you can check with our landlord" isn't a sufficient answer. Squatting for up to two weeks – sometimes longer – is legal on all land not otherwise posted. Chances of being prosecuted for trespassing are practically zero so long as there is no littering, open fires or vandalism; few land-owners wish to provoke people – too easy to set grudge fires. After several years experience we find we squat about 80% of the time; permission park about 20% of the time. (from VONU LIFE 73, March 1973, page 37)

EXCERPTS FROM JUNE 1973 LETTER

Yes, all our mail should now go to Berkeley. So far as I know there hasn't been problems with the Cave Junction Box since last Autumn, but we prefer to have an address out of the region. Besides the C.J. box is no longer ours & relaying mail has proven somewhat of a problem.

The impression I had of VONU LIFE when Lan first announced the split was that VONU LIFE would be a reprint of the best things from VONU LINK...

Later that Winter we did cross that particular creek in fairly high water by previously rigging line. I find I now tend to be more careful/conservative about natural hazard than when I was a weekend recreationist. This was demonstrated to me this Winter when I crossed that same creek without a rope but using a staff, carrying a backpack. Water was fairly high. I had feared that if I ever slipped & fell the increased water resistance would sweep me away. Well, the worst happened – both feet slipped at once & down I went – and simply sat there! My heavy back pack probably helped anchor me (dense load). I'm probably more conservative because of unavailability of medical aid, also because there is no status-game element of being daring.

I find I'm reluctant to delve into theoretical questions in strictly personal letters, preferring to write articles for wider circulation. This seems like more efficient communication but I'm not sure what it is. Your thoughts on ontogeny/phylogeny are interesting. My own thoughts on this aren't coherent yet. But the emotional reactions I had while writing "Rooting Out The Outposts" article in VONU LIFE 1973 support your hypothesis. On one hand, I had strong qualms about the article. On the other hand, I felt strongly enough that VL should include such an article that it be definitely published – charged against my advertising allotment if necessary (which I reserved for myself when I parted with VL). (This was probably unnecessary – Lan was short of material & kept soliciting more articles.) My feeling was that I didn't want VL to help clutter up the woods with statist clods. I didn't think the article would lead to the "conversion" of very many people, but that it would cause statist readers to turn off to wilderness vonu (if they were not turned off for other reasons – which seems more likely). So my article was an attempt to telescope movementism & vonuism. I'll be interested in any reactions as to how well it succeeded...

I never especially liked the word "freemate." But Roberta says she likes it, better than any other term she has heard (so do I) partly for lack of role playing element. We grabbed on to it when we wrote our "free marriage contract" (another term I don't especially like) because we couldn't think of anything better.

I don't think I could play a bludg convincingly & I'd hesitate to try, but suggestion is a good one. Having a fortnight instead of a week will allow starting off in a camp already set up, then people explore area, scout sites, discuss, scout some more, select site, move camp; then I try to find, & I have a camp for them to try & find – a continuing hide-and-seek game. This not a put-down of your suggestion. Nor is it to imply that there must be something wrong with someone who could play a bludg convincingly. I'm simply not a good actor.

[Editor's Note: This appears to be a discussion about how to improve the VONU WEEK program, indicating some intention to offer it again, at the time of this letter.]

LETTER TO ASE MAGAZINE, from Tom?

(Editor's Note: This is an obscure item: A letter appeared in July 1973 ALTERNATIVE SOURCES OF ENERGY MAGAZINE, unsigned, but I believe it may have been written by Tom. I base this conclusion on 3 clues: 1) writer mentions living in Siskiyou region, 2) address used is ALA, Box 91, Berkeley, CA 94701, which is the same address Tom uses in PACSCRIPT #1. 3) I recall that Tom was interested in developing hydroelectric power at his hidden camp, which was well within his abilities, since he was an electrical engineer. So the following <u>may</u> be Tom speaking:)

WATER POWER: "We have a site suitable for small hydroelectric power – about 100 foot head at 10 gallons per minute, which we would like to use to drive an automobile alternator and recharge batteries for a 12 volt electrical system.

A friend recommended that we use a carbon vane pump such as Airborne Sales #1191. Has any reader had experience doing this?

A problem we've run into is that the surplus houses, not only Airborne but Palley, are sold out of <u>carbon</u> vane pumps (which can handle water). Does anyone know of places which still handle these?

We'd also like suggestions as to the best alternator to use. We need one that's fairly small with low friction, perhaps from a foreign car, since at best we will be getting only 2 or 3 amps out.

We live in the Siskiyou region of northern California and would enjoy contacted other A.S.E. readers in the area. ALA, Box 91, Berkeley, CA 94701"

LETTER DATED September 14, 1973

My thinking has undergone major changes in the last several months on interfacing, "alternate economies," interrelations in general. Perhaps I am coming to the same conclusions you have – tho I'm not sure what yours are. I will probably write an article on subject when my thoughts become further crystallized.

The only person I've had good, deep, on-going theoretical discussions with is Roberta, because she is the only person I'm around enough to facilitate such discussions. Often thoughts/replies/answers will occur to me, not at the time of a conversation, but sometime later when I'm off by myself (similar to what you say happens with you), so I don't think one, or a few, intense, concentrated discussion sessions can provide the same opportunity as an on-going association. Several times we have visited and had long discussions with people who write theoretical articles, but the face-to-face was invariably limited to "nuts and bolts."

Berkeley address is still good.

LAST LETTER FROM TOM, February 14, 1974

I am now more eager to sell the 600 pound stash we have near Bella Coola. The woman who owns the farm on which they are stored is considering selling. There is no big hurry but I would like to dispose of the supplies by next summer at the latest. Also the chance that we will use them grows less. We would enjoy making another trip to that area (and the supplies give us a good excuse) but we have many projects we could better spend time on.

Your November 3rd letter, which we didn't get until a few weeks ago, because of misunderstanding with people receiving our mail, contained many interesting thoughts, as usual.

We withdrew from ATCOPS even before you did – irrelevant. My suggestion was to get out of ATCOPS, not out of silver. Without going to "unconventional" lengths, you could have bought bullion or coins from a local dealer and stored in a rented safety deposit box, for example. If you had asked what my recommendation would be if the only feasible alternatives were ATCOPS and a conventional savings account, my choice might have been different. Again, I didn't recommend against or for a particular form of investment: I passed along info I had received that ATCOPS's promoter was unreliable. I received a large manuscript detailing one person's experiences at ATCOPS. It is loaned out at the moment; I'll mail it to you when I get it back.

The last thing I recall writing on preserving savings was in VONU LIFE #6, page 8, was buying and storing silver coins.

I, too, am becoming very dubious as to the value of all "libertarian club" involvements, perhaps even more dubious than you. I still see some value for me in the kind of anonymous ideological/intellectual exchange which goes on in LIBERTARIAN CONNECTION, but we do not intend to use the "libertarian club" in the future as an avenue for gaining non-anonymous friends or associates.

Many more thoughts but not articulable yet.

(Editor's Note: ATCOPS, Atlantis Commodity Purchasing Service, was a silver bullion "bank," meant to be a forerunner to a Bank of Atlantis, which was a project of Operation Atlantis, an attempt to start a libertarian new country in the Caribbean. ATCOPS offered accounts denominated in decagrams of silver.

I believe the manuscript critical of ATCOPS mentioned above, was the one written by Pyro Egon, which I also received on loan, read, & returned.

Since this Feb. 74 letter was received, as far as I have been able to discover, no one has heard another word from, or about, Tom Marshall.)

THE DISAPPEARANCE

In a January 1986 letter, John Zube wrote to me from Australia:

"I still would like to know what happened to Tom Marshall and Roberta. Would they still live mainly in their secret dent? Do they have any children? Has he renounced his lifestyle, but does not want to recant publicly – or has his family possibly been found and wiped out by looters?"

I didn't have any answers for him then, and I don't know now, any more than Zube knows.

In the VONU BOOK 1, I wrote:

Rayo disappeared in 1974. I don't even know whether he is now dead or alive. We can only speculate about what might have happened to him. Perhaps one of his underground constructions fell in on him, or maybe he was eaten by a bear. Or he could have abandoned "vonu" and returned to a conventional lifestyle. Or maybe he moved overseas. Or perhaps he just decided that he would be freer if he broke off communication, and he is still out there in the mountains, living free.

If it were anyone else, I would guess that this complete silence over so many years must mean that he is dead. But Rayo is different because his goal always was to become invisible to coercers (meaning mainly Government). He might have come to believe that this required that he become invisible to everyone.

Now, many years later, I am more convinced than ever that Tom Marshall must be dead. I base that, not on any definite information that I have, but rather on the complete silence from or about him for so many years. When I began publishing material written by Tom, in the VONU BOOK and later, I had the thought that he might get in touch with me to complain about my appropriating his writing, if he was able to do so. But I never heard a word from him, or from Roberta, or from anyone representing either of them.

Most likely, he died in 1974 in unknown circumstances. His letters & articles in the years previous to that give no indication that he thought his end was near. He always spoke as if he had an indefinite future to look forward to. Moving his mailing address to Berkeley was a curious detail, but it did not seem to mean that he was no long living in Siskiyou. Whatever happened to Tom seemed to have been sudden & unexpected. That would suggest a fatal accident. But if Tom had contracted some fatal disease, it seems to me that he was the kind of person who wouldn't want to make a public announcement about it. He wouldn't want to evoke sympathy among his many admirers. People fawning over him is not something he would want. I'm familiar enough with certain characteristic details of his writing style that I'm sure I could recognize his writing if it had appeared in any libertarian publication even under a different name. But I have seen no such writing.

Tom Marshall's disappearance remains a complete mystery.

Appendix 1: Articles written by Tom Marshall in INNOVATOR

TM = signed Tom Marshall, ER = signed El Ray

- the nature and proper use of elections, TM, v1n1, p1-2, February 1964
- the Bahamas – a measure of freedom, TM, v1n2, p1-5, March 1964
- the time to design a free society, ER, v1n3, p1-11, April 1964
- what does "freedom" mean?, ER, v1n4, p1-16, May 1964
- champ – a village or a company?, ER, v1n5, p1-17, June 1964
- free trade zones – a bold solution for poverty, ER, v1n6, p1-22, July 1964
- "obscenity" and individual freedom, ER, v1n7, p1-25, August 1964
- how to develop liberty at a profit, ER, v2, p2-3, November 1964
- self-seeking (free isles), ER, p2-23, April 1965
- confidential subscription – a new service of INNOVATOR, by the General Manager (TM), p2-24, April 1965
- self-seeking (green revolution), ER, p2-27, May 1965
- self-seeking (take over a state), ER, p2-31, June 1965
- personal survival of nuclear attack, ER, p2-35, July 1965
- (reply concerning illegal activities), by the editor (TM), p2-39, August 1965
- i/t/a – alphabet of the future?, ER, p2-41, September 1965
- to the "mothers" of the Los Angeles riot, ER, p2-47, October 1965
- subscriber wins civil rights case, editor (TM), p2-48, October 1965
- self-seeking (mass movements), ER, p2-49, October 1965
- agoric incentives supercede hierarchic controls, ER, p3-1, November 1965
- self-seeking (ethical enclave), ER, p3-3, November 1965
- victory on a great frontier, editor (TM), p3-4, November 1965
- philosophy of INNOVATOR, editor (TM), p3-8, December 1965
- a penny saved...? (short item), ER, p3-13, February 1966
- self-seeking (take over a state), ER, p3-42, August 1966

- depression? hyperinflation? collapse?, ER, p4-15, February 1967
- self-seeking (internationally mobile), ER, p4-21, March 1967
- passage without passport, ER, p4-23, March 1967
- reviews 2 items "on the market," ER, p4-27, April 1967
- start your own underground bank, "name withheld" but sounds like TM, p4-31, May 1967
- profit in paper (books), ER, p4-31, May 1967
- bella coola journey, TM, p4-48, September 1967
- proposal for a clandestine communications net, "name withheld," maybe TM, p4-52, October 1967
- ER listed as issue editor, March 1968
- letter from a nomad, "name withheld, p6-1, March 1968
- buying a mobile home, TM, p6-1, March 1968
- visit to libervan, ER & Amelia Eiland, p6-3, March 1968
- mobility – an alternate retreat concept, ER, p6-9, April 1968
- ER listed as issue editor, Winter 1969 (W69)
- editorial: on strategy of cultural change, ER, p7-27, W69
- refuting the tax myths, ER, p7-27, W69
- bring it home free, TM, p7-28, W69
- arbitration clause for free market contracts, ER, p7-29, W69
- save for liberty, TM, p7-30, W69
- banking in Switzerland, "name withheld," p7-33, W69
- issue your own play money (short item), ER, p7-34, W69
- self-liberation ways: a compilation and evaluation, ER, p7-44, Spring 1969
- ER and the Gatherer, issue editors, Autumn 1969
- America: loath it & leave it (new country projects), TM, p7-71, A69
- further report from a nomad, "name withheld," p7-76, A69
- more self-liberation ways, ER, p7-78, A69
- surmounting barriers to freedom, ER, p7-79, A69

total 46 articles, excluding a couple short items.

Appendix 2: Articles written by Tom Marshall in VONU LIFE 1973 the special handbook issue, all except one signed "Rayo"

- ecology, peace, vonu, technology, p2
- 16 ways to live freer, a critical evaluation, p3
- 40 by 8 feet of shelter for $30 and one day, p13
- how to build and design with natural timbers, p16
- warmth without fire, complete plans for a $55 foam hut, p29
- warmth without fire, stephenson's tent liner, p35
- choosing a van for living aboard, p37
- bring it home free, by T, p81 (reprinted from W69 INNOVATOR where the author listed is Tom Marshall)
- what is big brother watching, p89
- fallout detector, p92
- teaching reading at home, a simple unique way, p93
- troglodyte community, p98
- smumans, the super hobos, p101
- ethical land use, p105
- rooting out the outposts, p109
- surmounting personal obstacles to vonu, p114

Total 16 articles. There are also 13 unsigned articles. Some of them may have been written by Tom Marshall. And the longest article is "Far out eating for $10 a month," 36 pages long, starting at p41, signed Haelen Hygeia, which is a pen name used by Roberta. There were some other articles written by other persons, notably Al Fry and Paul Doerr, and one by me, Jim Stumm, signed "Lysander," but Tom and Roberta wrote most of VL 73.

Get Shane Radliff's book and learn about alternative lifestyles in pursuance of freedom!

WWW.TINYURL.COM/SELFLIBERATE1

Get #agora, a terrific crypto-agorist novella and follow Daniel LaRusso's journey into the world of agorism, crypto-anarchy, and freedom!

WWW.TINYURL.COM/AGORAanarchy

Additional Resources

- **The Vonu Podcast**: If you want to learn more about anything covered in this book, I'd highly recommend you check out the podcast Kyle Rearden and I do. In season 1, we covered the philosophy of vonu, season 2 was the practice of vonu, and the current season, 3, is where we develop and update vonu to the modern day.
  o   www.vonupodcast.com
- **Vonu: The Search for Personal Freedom, Number 2 – Letters from Rayo**
  o   www.vonupodcast.com/vonu2
- **Vonulife, March 1973 (Special Edition)**
  o   www.vonupodcast.com/vl
- **Ocean Freedom Notes**
  o   www.vonupodcast.com/ofn
- **Self-Liberation Notes**
  o   www.vonupodcast.com/sln
- **Going Mobile**
  o   www.vonupodcast.com/gm
- **Low-Cost Living**
  o   www.vonupodcast.com/lcl
- **Dwelling Portably [sic]**
  o   www.vonupodcast.com/dp
- **Articles About Vonu**
  o   www.vonupodcast.com/vonuarticles
- **Liberty Under Attack**: If you're seeking out paths to personal freedom, then you need to check out The Freedom Umbrella of Direct Action and the Direct Action Series.
  o   www.libertyunderattack.com/FUDA
  o   www.libertyunderattack.com/DAS
- **The Last Bastille Blog**: This is Kyle's blog and it's chockful of incredible, highly valuable information. He has written over 150 book reviews, a couple books pertinent to vonu, and much more.
  o   www.thelastbastille.com
- **YouTube**: If you're pursuing any of the lifestyle changes or strategies I covered above, then YouTube will be your best

friend. Recommended search terms: "van dwelling," "living aboard a boat," "minimalist sailboating," etc.

Support Us

If you enjoyed the book and found it valuable, please consider making a bitcoin donation!

Bitcoin: 15Bdzduwt92jYFGFaK2NSkPYFTaLbtonJg